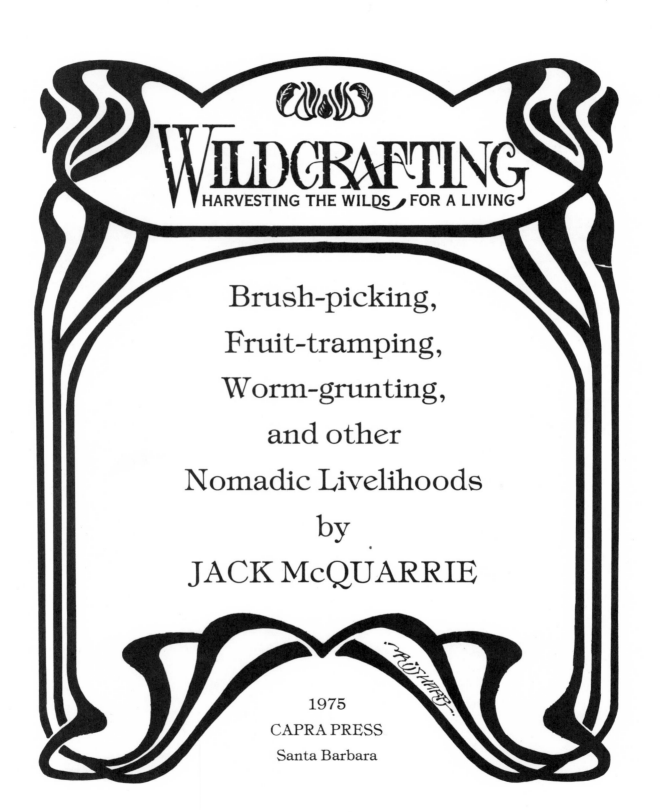

WILDCRAFTING
HARVESTING THE WILDS FOR A LIVING

Brush-picking,
Fruit-tramping,
Worm-grunting,
and other
Nomadic Livelihoods
by
JACK McQUARRIE

1975
CAPRA PRESS
Santa Barbara

Composition by Mackintosh Typography, Santa Barbara.
Printed and bound by Banta West in the United States of America.

LIBRARY OF CONGRESS CATALOGING IN PUBLICATION DATA

McQuarrie, Jack, 1937-
    Wildcrafting : harvesting the wilds for a living.

    1.   Gleaning—United States.   2.   Migrant agricultural
laborers—United States.   I. Title.
HD1549.M3   338.1   75-27669
ISBN 0-88496-042-0

CAPRA PRESS
631 State Street, Santa Barbara, CA 93101

Table of Contents

Marie's Foreword

It's an exhilarating experience to maneuver a ladder skillfully among the snarly branches of a massive cherry tree, or to hike out of the deep forest with a hefty bale of greenery on your back. Working outdoors helps build physical strength which I find brings a surge of self-confidence.

Few jobs available to women in our culture permit us to function fully as people, challenging both mind and body. We were taught that the female is the "weaker sex." Sadly, we accepted this myth and have not ventured into those few occupations which develop strength and independence.

Working in the orchards and forests has made a strong and happy impression upon me. Learning the identity of wild plants and trees has been a source of pride and, for me, of far more value than all paperwork I learned in my earlier days.

A love of the outdoors is a passion shared by nearly all the women we've encountered in our travels. In the shade on a hot afternoon as friendships blossom and intimacies are shared, a deeper motivation emerges—a thirst for adventure and new experience (lucky is she whose mate share such cravings), traits that are commonly attributed only to the male. The women we meet speak of their inability to tolerate being boxed in by traditional lifestyles for any length of time, and they speak too of the loneliness, isolation and lack of pride so often felt by the housewife, who must depend upon someone else for her livelihood.

Economic independence and a simple "urge to see the country at my own pace" is the refrain we often hear from the increasing numbers of single women we meet on harvest roads each year. They have good reasons— one being that equality of pay and recognition have long been a reality in many rural occupations. Being paid according to the amount you harvest insures this. Also, as you develop skills with tools and machinery, you are encouraged to use them. You are as likely to see a female as a male driving a tractor through the orchard, or trucking produce to the packing house.

I don't want to mislead female readers. Sexism does rear its head occasionally. Sometimes there is the camp braggart who boasts how he made over a hundred dollars that day, omitting the fact that his wife and children were picking with him and the family total was that much.

Jack and I take turns at the campfire when we must, but we've found that in most small towns near harvest areas there is at least one cafe that serves hearty meals at prices working people can afford. By retreating to the camaraderie of cafes for supper, we escape the fuss and bother of cooking, and enjoy ourselves. For us, it's a good life.

—Marie McQuarrie

Introduction

This book is for you who feel at home in the wilds and orchards of America, have gypsy in your heart, and respect for the natural cycles of growth and harvest. If you favor canyons of spruce and fir to those of steel and glass, if a wild meadow means more than a front yard lawn, and if you have an eye for hidden herbs and ripening berries, then this book should serve you well. It tells you how to live at your own pace in the wilderness, harvesting things that have a market—nuts, berries, foliage, seeds, and crude drugs. Nature is bountiful wherever you want to be—in the forests of the Pacific Northwest, the Appalachian woods, Southern swamps, Southwest deserts—you can dig, prune, peel, or shake the trees. With a strap of iron you can even play a tune on a driven stake and lure a wiggling harvest into your hands. The point is, you can earn necessary cash in the countryside with little more than a pair of hands and an appreciation of nature.

If you live in the city and enjoy a vacation in the Great Outdoors, you can earn your travel expenses by harvesting as you go. Sometimes the whole family can help. If you already live in the country and it's off-season for your crops, you can heal a wounded budget by collecting in the nearest woods. If you want to explore, answer to no one, and earn a full livelihood, you can do that too. In any case, you will be close to nature where the air is good and peace is golden.

It's not entirely idyllic, of course. The desert sun can be merciless, northwest storms can burst upon you, mosquitoes and sidewinders can plague you, as well as thorns, nettles, blistered feet and aching backs. Jack McQuarrie points out that while wildcrafting isn't easy at first—it takes a while to get the hang of it, to learn certain dexterities and logistics—there is no one need to push. Go easy, he says, no one is driving you, find your comfortable limits. Your rewards will equal your diligence.

7

Jack and Marie McQuarrie have interesting lives, a cross of country and urban, dividing their time between wildcrafting on the road and living in a small city. Twelve years ago he worked his way through college by brushpicking in the Northwest. Afterwards he led a conventional life with a number of jobs, mainly newspaper and magazine reporting, with a mortgage to meet and boxed into the frustrations of earning and spending without much freedom. Forty hours a week, fifty weeks a year seemed too dear a price for mundane survival. One summer he and Marie revisited the brushpicking country of his student days, had a happy time in the forest, and earned enough to cover their vacation expenses. A few years later, on another holiday trip, their car broke down and so ruined the health of their pocketbook that they were ready to cut their vacation short and hightail it home. They happened to read an article in the "Portland Journal" announcing the opening of the cherry harvest in the Hood River area. They joined the pickers and seven days later held $200 in their purple fingers—not bad for beginners.

That convinced them there was nothing to stop them from traveling almost anywhere, anytime, if they were willing to work along the way. Gypsy wanderings became a way of life. With a tank of gas and some loose change, the McQuarries could hit the road confident of earning their way, of befriending freer spirits than they meet in other walks of life, and finding simplicity and peace. They feel emancipated from the compulsive consumerism, happy to be free, in their hearts, from those aspects of civilization that Mark Twain described as "a limitless multiplication of unnecessary necessaries."

"It's so different now," McQuarrie told us. "In earlier years when vacation time came, I'd go through a stack of traveler's checks and come home rather depressed. For one thing, I felt quite insulated from the real essence of other places and people, a feeling you never get when you're working your way. And I'd realize that the adventures I'd paid for and traveled far for, weren't essentially much different than those we could've had a couple of miles from home."

The work styles described in this book don't apply exclusively to nomads, however. Some of the occupations can sustain people as long as they want to stay in some very beautiful regions of North America.

These days many people are going back to the country. Even living off the land requires some money. There are years when bugs will thwart the most conscientious gardener, some groceries must be bought in the winter since even the most spartan palate will tire of a Gibbons' diet of wild hickory nuts and dandelion shoots. Even jalopies need parts. The homesteader can do many things depending upon where he lives—peel cascara bark, dig ginseng, "grunt" for earthworms, pick decorative foliage, gather wild nuts and berries, or pick orchard fruit. The list is long. An outdoor harvest of some kind can be found in the countryside nearly everywhere on the North American continent.

It may be hard to believe, in these days of high unemployment, that there is a limited labor supply for many of the harvests described herein. According to the Department of Agriculture in "A Guide to Medicinal Plants of Appalachia," ". . . during the past 30 to 50 years, fewer and fewer people have been harvesting wild plants in Appalachia . . . mainly because of families moving to more prosperous areas. Between 1950 and 1960, the southern Appalachian region lost through emigration more than a million people, nearly a fifth of the population. Increases in local blue-collar employment opportunities, a growing reluctance to work in the fields and forests . . . have also reduced the natural plant harvests for drug materials."

There are advantages to swimming upstream, as McQuarrie tells us. If you head for the country while everyone else is fleeing to the city, you will have less competition, and the wild crops will be fuller.

William Cooper wrote in his "Guide to the Wilderness:" "It is not large funds that are wanted, but a constant supply, like a small stream that never dies. To have a great capital is not so necessary as to know how to manage a small one and never to be without a little." Wildcrafting can be a small, everlasting stream. You can work at it as casually as you will, according to your needs, knowing it is always there. Fruit-tramping, for example, has become a popular alternative workstyle. The McQuarries met scores of first-timers in the orchards last year, with the same incentive as the veterans—to build a poke sufficient to carry them through the winter months.

Few realize that the forests offer a livelihood to people not in the timber industry. Yet the Forest Service estimates that the collecting of forest greens and crude drugs last year provided harvesters in Oregon and Washington about $15 million. It's provided a principal income for many rural families, and supplements thousands of others—loggers, fishermen, farmers, and housewives. Experienced brushpickers have little trouble earning more than $40 a day.

Beginners, of course, won't do nearly as well. McQuarrie suggests they should first find a buyer and reach an understanding about collecting procedures and prices which are determined by quality, distance from markets, supply and demand. They are advised to submit small quantities the first few times, until they get the hang of it. Outlets for many forest products are often located in the principal collecting areas. The yellow pages often carry their names.

McQuarrie came through Santa Barbara to drop off his last chapter. He was heading north for a few weeks of cascara bark peeling and then will pick up the cherry harvest in Oregon. He had an uneasy look on his face. "I just hope I've made two things clear," he said. "First, that people don't get the idea they can go out and harvest anywhere they please—in many places they must have permissions and permits. And the second thing is, that they have consideration for nature and don't go tearing into the forest like butchers. Tell them the more good judgment they use, the more there will be to harvest next year. Man and nature need each other. Pruning salal, for example, is beneficial to both. I've tried to say that in my chapters and I hope the readers listen."

Those two cautions are well-taken. Harvesters should get permission from landowners and remember that collecting in national parks and some state parks is strictly forbidden. On other public lands where harvesting is allowed, permits are often necessary—many are free and some require a small fee. For information concerning permits, consult local forestry offices, state conservation agencies, county extension agents and other Department of Agriculture representatives.

At this moment Jack and Marie McQuarrie must be making their gypsy camp near the Eel River. He's probably honing his cascara spud and sipping coffee made from stream water. While I'm listening to the State Street river of workers driving home.

—Leon Elder

WILDCRAFTING

Brush-Picking

The hulking figure with the massive "head" who sometimes startles folk in the woods of the Pacific Northwest, who lumbers awkwardly through the undergrowth and is even mistaken for Big Foot—this hoarse-breathing, two-legged creature is actually a brushpicker laboring under a mass of forest greenery. He's become a common sight in that region most of the year. Relatively unheralded, brushpicking is a most enjoyable forest occupation. It is simply the harvesting of foliage from the understory of certain plants and bushes that thrive in the lush coastal forests of southern British Columbia, Washington, Oregon and northern California.

Although these plants are often considered as no more than impeding weeds by loggers and hunters, they are highly prized by the florist trade; particularly salal, evergreen huckleberry and sword fern. Free of blight and insect damage, sprays from these plants become backgrounds in wreaths, bouquets and floral arrangements.

Some years ago brushpicking helped put me through college. Since then I have often used these skills to underwrite a vacation in the Pacific Northwest where there are many buyers of forest shrubbery who operate processing plants in the area. Names and addresses are listed at the end of this chapter.

Last summer I revisited my home town, Powell River, B.C., and found two old friends, Ray Leach and Phil Jamieson, still brushpicking full time. They have even expanded their operations by renting a shed and installing a sprinkling system. (Keeping forest greenery cool and moist is imperative.) In the shed they wrap bundles of wild brush in polyethylene and pack them in corrugated boxes, 20 at a time. Twice a week they load the cases onto their pickup and drive to the local freight yard where the greens are shipped, via refrigerated truck, to a Vancouver distributor.

My friends have been picking brush for over 15 years and know the forest greens business inside and out. Because of their expertise, they are able to perform several essential operations while picking in the forest—gauging the proper weight of a bundle, grading it, and wiring the stems. Less-skilled brushpickers must rely upon packing plant operators like Phil and Ray to do this for them.

I asked them what good words they might have for the would-be brushpicker. "A newcomer, who must rely upon a middleman, will likely earn $10 to $15 a day for the first few months," said Phil. "But after that a person should average $25 to $30."

Most packing plant operators are eager to find new pickers. The demand for wild brush is high and, naturally, the more they ship the more they make. Phil says that anyone interested in brushpicking should first speak to a packer and ask to be shown the ropes. "If we're tied up and can't take a new picker out ourselves, we can arrange for him or her to accompany another experienced collector."

Phil advises the newcomer not to be discouraged the first few times out. A beginner may pick a lot of inferior material that must be culled leaving him with only a few dollars to show for a day's work. He'll be angry at himself, as well as the packers for being "too fussy." But if he hangs in there for a few days the work will get easier and he'll gain a clear appreciation for the money-making potential of brushpicking.

"Take heart," says Phil. "About all you need is a jalopy that will ride high enough to navigate the rutty, ungraded forest roads, and a bit of light rope for binding the brush into bundles." Brushpicking is essentially simple and menial once the basics are learned. Phil recalls an eager gent who pulled up at his packing plant in his pickup loaded high with entire salal bushes, roots and all. "He said he had a lot of salal for us and asked for a pitchfork. When we told him we couldn't use it, he drove off in disgust, presumably to the town dump."

The proper way to harvest salal and huckleberry is by hand, snapping off the sprays neatly. These sprays must be unmarred, flat, fan-shaped and 12 to 30 inches long. These are trimmed, and collected in one hand with the leaves laid together as flat as possible. Buyers prefer that at least one-third of the sprays in each bunch be of maximum length, while the rest are laid together in gradually declining lengths. The shorter pieces include a few single stems and are usually trimmings from the longer sprays. Responsible brushpickers leave smaller sprays on the bush to grow another year.

Gathered correctly, a 1 5/8 lb. handful of salal brings a picker between 40 and 50 cents, depending upon crop and market conditions. Although huckleberry brings a nickel

less, it is considered a better money-maker than salal because it is more brittle and snaps off easier, making faster picking.

The trick is in learning to recognize marketable sprays in what the untrained eye sees as a tangled thicket. The eyes of veteran pickers are always a spray or two ahead of their hands. These pros can go into an inferior or worked-over patch and still make good wages. The dream of the novice, cousin of the hidden-treasure seeker, is to find the rich virgin patch. I've known many such dreamers who spent most of the day tramping through the woods seeking the ideal patch, and by evening wondering why they didn't make nearly as much as the veterans.

When you watch experts like Phil and Ray work through the forest, it's easy to get excited by what they're earning. It takes each man only about two minutes to tack a new bundle, wire twisted around the snapped stems, to a nearby tree where it can be easily seen and collected later on the way out. These bunches are then grouped into "double-end bales" for hauling to the truck. These are made by laying a length of strong twine on

the ground in a straight line. The stems of the bunches, three at a time, are laid on the twine, in alternating directions. The bales usually contain 30 to 40 bunches, although some eager-beavers will tie 50 together. The big bale, resembling a green haystack, is then hoisted atop shoulders and hauled, sometimes for a considerable distance, to the branch road and the waiting "bush buggy." After the first 50 yards even a moderate bale can get heavy and is the main reason you rarely see a brushpicker with weight problems.

Evergreen Huckleberry
(vaccinium ovatum)

A shrub that grows 4 to 8 feet high and bears oval-shaped, finely-toothed leaves about 3/4 to 1 1/2 inches in length, is valued almost as much for its clusters of edible berries as for its greenery. Experienced brushpickers say that the best huckleberry sprays are usually found within five miles of salt water, under a forest canopy that permits filtered light. Bushes growing in the open generally lack good form and color.

Each year, about 80 percent of the huckleberry foliage that goes to market is harvested in Washington, most of it from the Puget Sound Basin. The bulk of the B.C. crop (about 15 percent of the annual total) is concentrated on Texada Island, a few miles off the Powell River.

Salal
(gaultheria shallon)

A shrub bearing smooth and leathery leaves that are oval-shaped and from 2 to 4 inches in length, like huckleberry, grows best under partially shaded conditions near salt water. The best salal is usually found in an area of lightly stocked coniferous trees. Most of last year's harvest of salal (almost 3 million bunches) was taken from Washington and B.C.

Sword Fern
(polystickum munitum)

The third most sought-after forest green in the Pacific Northwest, achieves its best growth in regions that have heavy rainfall and deep, fertile soils. It is often found under older stands of fir, hemlock and spruce. Much of the annual harvest of sword fern comes from the rain forests of Oregon and Washington.

The techniques for harvesting sword ferns are unlike those for salal and huckleberry. As fern fronds are generally too tough and stringy to break off easily by hand, most professional pickers use a small, curved knife attached to a ring that fits over a finger. Fronds are cut to length with the ring knife, handles made by stripping three inches of leaflets at the stem, and placed one at a time in the picker's free hand. A piece of strong twine is then cinched around the stems. Often, the frond tips in each bunch fan out; this is corrected before baling by rearranging each tip so that it lies directly on top of the others.

"Regular bunches" of sword fern are in greatest demand—these contain 52 near-perfect fronds 25 to 28 inches in length. A lesser demand exists for "long bunches" containing 22 fronds 31 to 33 inches in length. At present, sword fern harvesters earn about 25 cents a bundle. To be marketable, ferns must be relatively free of insect and disease damage and without torn or missing petals.

Scotch Broom

Besides the "big three" of the wild floral greens, there is an intermittent demand for a few others. One is Scotch broom (cytisus scoparius), distinguished by its slender, green-stemmed spikes bearing tiny trifoliate leaves and, during springtime, bright yellow flowers. An aggressive plant which thrives under open, difficult conditions, it is harvested in limited quantities near the coast of southwestern Oregon and southern Puget Sound, November through January.

Scotch broom is picked in pieces 30 to 40 inches long and made into two pound bunches by the processor for shipment. Each bunch earns the picker 20 cents. The plant is also harvested commercially along the eastern seaboard, but the collecting season is shorter and the quality lower than on the West Coast.

The increased demand for Scotch broom, a native of Europe, is small but steady, due to the present use of spiky foliage inside a bouquet, rather than behind it for background effect.

Another trend in floral designing — toward shorter bouquets requiring shorter background foliage — has created an increased demand for short bunches of salal and huckleberry. Sometimes called "Little Johns," these are worth about 15 cents less than regular bunches to the collector.

False Boxwood

Another plant sometimes used in floral arrangements is false boxwood (pachistima myrsinites), a small-leafed evergreen shrub found in the mountains of the Pacific Northwest. About 40,000 bundles of this plant, similar to huckleberry in appearance, is harvested in B.C. each year for local use.

Dwarf Oregon Grape
(mahonia nervosa)

A short forest shrub with holly-like leaves, is occasionally sought by wilderness harvesters —

usually near the coast in Washington and the northern Willamette Valley in Oregon.

Whatever plant species the brushpicker collects, there are certain procedures to follow. To protect their bundles from heating up and "shattering" — that is, shedding their leaves — wise harvesters deliver their greenery to the processor as soon as possible after picking. Since all wild floral greens are most vulnerable to deterioration between the time they are picked and their deposit in a shower room or cold storage, brushpickers while in the forest are careful to keep their bundles in shaded areas.

Brushpickers sensitive to their environment are careful to collect modest amounts from each plant. One-fourth of the foliage of forest plants may be harvested without harmful effects — in fact, the plant will usually benefit from the "pruning." In any event, if only marketable sprays are plucked, there is little danger of injuring the plant.

If you decide to become a brushpicker, you will soon be made aware of certain risks and aggravations. These include nature's booby traps — you'll swear they were set by woodland guerrillas just for you — gnarled roots above ground, stumps and camouflaged holes. Any of these can send both you and your precious bale flying. You'll pick yourself up cussing, praying that your greens haven't been bruised too badly and won't have to be culled later in the plant. And all your bundles, if they haven't been wired securely enough, will have to be rebaled on the spot. But console yourself if you weren't hurt that you had sense enough to let go of the bale on your way down.

Brushpickers seldom go out alone. Besides the danger of being hurt there is always the possibility of getting lost. You'd be surprised how easy it is to get turned around in the forest when your mind is on other matters. If you do go into the bush alone, it's advisable to leave bright cloth markers on trees and stumps along your trail. Brushpickers do a lot of yelling in the woods, one reason why they are often considered a species of animal or madman. We like to think a bit of whooping helps keep us in touch with each other.

As far as animals go, they are as wary as we are. I've surprised many deer. Black bear are occasionally encountered, but brushpickers and bears have an equal aversion to each other and are both eager to get distance between them. I've seen the spoor of cougars but have yet to catch sight of those shy cats. Poisonous snakes don't seem to inhabit the same terrain as salal and huckleberry. While I've never worried about four-legged creatures, two-legged varmints are another matter. The longest picking days I've ever spent were during the fall hunting season. Hunting (excuse my prejudice) is a sport that seems super-saturated with idiocy. Far too many hunters have few qualms about shooting in the proximity of others, who may or may not be in the line of fire. A young Vancouver Island brushpicker was killed by a careless hunter a few years ago. You will find that brushpickers do much more vocalizing during hunting season and take to wearing brightly colored hats or jackets.

There are only two months of the year when salal and huckleberry can't be picked—May and June, when the new growth needs to harden. But that's no reason to forego wages then. There are still sword ferns to gather. Some B.C. brushpickers head for the interior to harvest boxwood. One told me, "we have to work harder to make money at these, but the important thing is that we're never out of work."

Those who gather brush year-round are a special breed, unlikely to be deterred by the cold and wet. During bad weather, intrepid collectors don protective apparel— rain-proof suits, mackinaws, gum-boots, heavy woolen socks and warm toques. Their penchant to dress for comfort and safety, rather than fashion, often gives them a ludicrous look.

Snow doesn't stop the dedicated brushpicker. Tall trees shelter many of the patches and where it doesn't you just brush off the snow and keep going. Brushpickers only stay out of the woods during periods of prolonged, severe freezing—frozen leaves will turn black when handled.

A surprising number of patches grow near the road, one reason why brushpicking is a popular family pursuit in the Northwest. In Powell River entire families spend exhilarating days together outdoors brushpicking, and whetting a keen appetite for joyous picnics. Husband-wife brushpicking teams are a natural. I know several and they're doing very well, both on and off the job. This says something for being outdoors, free from the modern-day pressure cooker, and working together for the daily bread.

Things are still unstructured in B.C. as far as brushpicking is concerned, but in recent years there has been a tendency for forest harvesters in Washington and Oregon to enter into leasing agreements with the government, companies and private individuals. In some cases, pickers pay landowners from one to five cents a bunch, depending upon the accessibility and quality of the forest crop; harvesting rights are also sold on an acreage basis.

Brushpicking may be news to you, but that isn't because it's new. Back in 1915 Sam Roake of Castle Rock, Washington, gathered sword ferns for local florists. A few years later, George Kirk of Tacoma began pakcing and shipping sword ferns for a national market.

In 1925, Joe Evans of Bandon, Oregon, who had been harvesting small quantities of huckleberry brush for florists in the Midwest, shipped a

case to the Kervan Company, a large New York distributor of floral greenery. Jack Kervan, who had ordered the brush after a trip to the Pacific Northwest in search of new varieties of backdrop material, wrote: "I felt that this type of hucklebrush would go over . . . I had no idea the response would be so tremendous."

When Isaac and Henry Callison of Aberdeen, Washington—who had supplied the eastern pharmaceutical trade with cascara bark for several years—learned of the burgeoning demand for huckleberry foliage from the Pacific Northwest, they immediately began to recruit pickers. By the early 30's, the elder Callisons and their offspring were well-established in the picking and packing of huckleberry. So was George Kirk, who had also expanded his business. A few years later, these two firms—which still dominate the market in the Northwest—also began to process salal when it became popular with eastern florists.

There was plenty of brush for these two growing firms, as well as for the numerous small, independent packers that began to spring up to meet the increasing demand. Soon harvesters, an ample supply guaranteed by a depressed economy, were bringing tons of greenery into the processing plants.

Today, the picking, packing and shipping of forest brush involves thousands of workers in the Pacific Northwest. Bundles of greenery go out from this region by the refrigerated truck load to florists throughout North America.

The economic importance of the brushpicking industry today is indicated by the Forest Service estimate that "the harvesting of floral greenery provides about two and a half million dollars a year to pickers in the Pacific Northwest."

The appeal brushpicking has for many is probably due more to the nature of the work than to dollars. There's much to be said for working in shaded forest glens, far removed from urbania, hearing the whispering of a fresh wind through tall evergreens, the raucous insults of an angry jay, the crashings of a startled deer.

This work attracts "a special breed of cat," according to Cecil Callison, president of I.P. Callison and Sons Inc. "They are very independent and work when they want to work. They often take along a fishing pole and just stop and fish when they feel like it."

Buyers: The following are the major buyers of wild forest greens in the Pacific Northwest. Callison is the largest, with 18 packing plants scattered throughout B.C., Oregon and Washington, followed by The Kirk Company. In addition to these four firms, there are several smaller independent packers.

I.P. Callison and Sons Inc.
Lloyd Building
Seattle, Wa 98101

The Kirk Company
615 E. Pioneer Ave.
Puyallup, Wa 98371

Pacific Coast Evergreens
Head of Bay
Bremerton, Wa 98310

Hiawatha Inc.
526 S. First St.
Shelton, Wa 98584

Processing plants for floral greenery, brush, and cascara bark in the Pacific Northwest. (Indicated by nearest cities.)

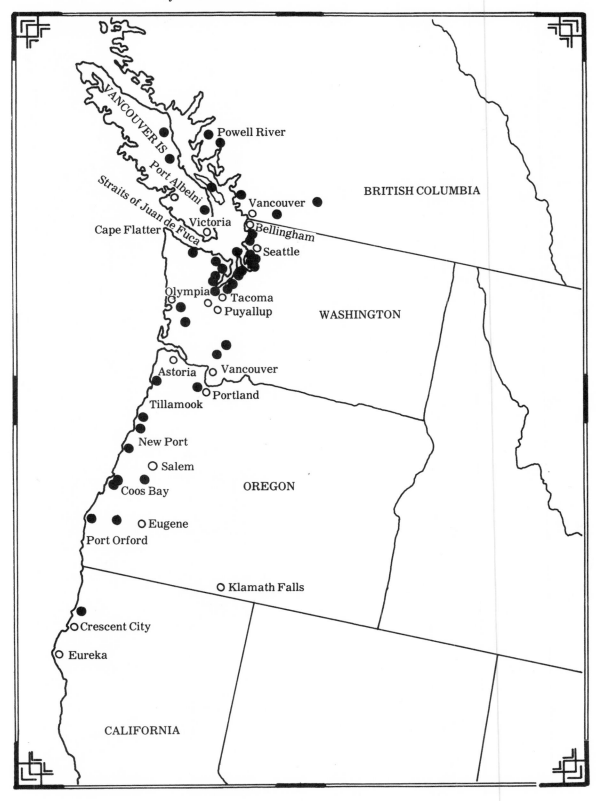

Gathering
Forest Decoratives

Galax

Stalking through forest glens in search of decorative plant life is an activity profitably pursued in several regions of North America. Nowhere else is the collecting of forest greenery more avid than in the southern Appalachian mountains, where the most sought-after plants, galax, leucothoe and mountain laurel, are generally harvested from September through April.

Gathering these decoratives allows Appalachian families to supplement annual incomes by as much as $1,000 to $2,000. One elderly woman in the Mount Mitchell area of North Carolina told us that she consistently made over $1,000 a year harvesting galax on her own, working three days a week for the nine-month picking period.

Many galax harvesters we met earned over $30 a day. We didn't fare so well in the few days we spent collecting, together averaging slightly over $20 daily, but we weren't as diligent as we could have been either—for us, it was enough to have discovered another pleasant, outdoor livelihood.

Galax (galax aphylla) is a distinctive evergreen plant. Its leaves are heart-shaped, leathery and toothed, with long and slender petioles; in the fall, its color changes from a rich green to maroon. The creamy white flowers of this plant blossom in long dense spikes. Galax grows best in partial shade and is usually found in patches, either in the clearings or edges of dense forests, in a range extending from the southern boundary of Pennsylvania to Alabama and Georgia. Conservation-minded galax harvesters avoid picking the leaves during the growing season, when the petiole isn't easily separated from the root. Irresponsible harvesters can destroy entire beds of galax.

Most galax harvesters carry large burlap bags over their shoulders, stuffed with the leaves they pick. We found our orange-picking bags ideal for this purpose. Once collected, galax leaves must be sorted according to size and color and then tied into bunches of 25. These graded bunches are then packed into cardboard boxes and sold to dealers in floral greenery. There are several in the southern Appalachian regions—especially in western North Carolina and southwestern Virginia, the center of the market area. We encountered especially large local industries near Burnsville and Marion, North Carolina. Galax is widely used as a base or background material for floral arrangements, and the leaves are favored in Christmas decorations.

Leucothoe Plant

The sprays of the leucothoe plant (leucothoe editorum) are also collected and marketed in large numbers in the southern Appalachians. This evergreen shrub is also known as dog-hobble, ivy, switch ivy, and poison hemlock (because cattle that eat the leaves in early spring can get fatally sick). Leucothoe reaches a height of three to six feet and has slightly curved branches bearing lustrous green leaves which are lance-shaped, spiny-toothed and sport conspicuous petioles about half an inch long. The flower spikes have an attractive creamy or pinkish color, but a rather unpleasant odor. Leucothoe is found in southern mountain areas,

Galax (aphylla), an evergreen perennial, is a low-growing, stemless plant forming leafy clumps up to 6 inches high from underground runners.

Leucothoe (editorum) has evergreen leaves up to six inches long. The flower buds are naked through winter, white blossoms when in bloom.

26

from Virginia to Georgia, usually in beds bordering small streams, or in other damp areas.

Collectors cut leucothoe sprays into lengths from 10 to 20 inches and, like galax, carry them in burlap sacks slung around their shoulders. Also like galax, these are later tied in bunches of 25, put in containers and sold to local dealers, who ship them throughout the country. Leucothoe harvesting has its discouraging aspects. For one, deer are as fond of the plant as harvesters are; these animals can leave vast areas devoid of salable sprays. Another disadvantage is the effect the plant has on some people — causing skin rash and sometimes headaches.

Mountain Laurel

The third major marketable Appalachian forest decorative is mountain laurel (kalmia latifolia), which commonly grows in thickets as tall as 20 feet; it is further recognized by its evergreen, elliptical and leathery leaves. Although mountain laurel ranges from Canada to Florida, it is most common in the southern Appalachians, where it grows so dense that it is hard for young trees to compete. Stems cut near the ground will readily sprout and new material can be harvested from the same stem for many years. This holds true for most forest decoratives collected for market.

The southern Appalachians and the Pacific Northwest are the primary sources of marketable forest greenery, but by no means the only ones. Harvesters of greenery for the floral industry are working in most of North America's forests — particularly near Christmas time when the demand is highest. Three of the most popular are evergreen boughs, holly and mistletoe.

Mistletoe

Mistletoe is an especially good income-producer during the Christmas season. Most plant manuals claim its range is from southern New Jersey and southern Pennsylvania through Appalachia to the Gulf states and west to Kansas and Texas. But I have seen it hanging on west coast trees as well and can surmise that mistletoe grows almost everywhere.

Mistletoe is a parasitic plant that grows on the trunks and branches of a great variety of trees. It is very conspicuous on hardwoods when they have lost their leaves, but I have also spotted it on apple trees in Washington's Yakima Valley and on the alders and junipers of southeastern Oregon. One of the few generalizations that can be made is that it prefers trees that are open-grown or bordering the edge of a dense forest. The entire plant is picked, but the sprigs with flowers or fruit generally bring the highest prices. Mistletoe can occasionally be picked from the ground but is usually found at higher reaches and collectors must climb the trees, or shoot it down with shotguns. If you harvest mistletoe from precarious perches, it's advisable to have a sack or bag of some kind strapped over a shoulder holding a bounty. Here again, we've found our fruit-picking bags handy. The pickings in your bag can get scrunched up while knocking around a tree, however. To avoid this, try another method—bring an old sheet and have two people hold it as a net below while you drop your sprigs into it. Those who consider tree-climbing as risky as sky-diving and Russian roulette might prefer to use ladders and long-handled tree trimmers to get mistletoe.

Mistletoe is a parasite that sometimes smothers the trees it frequents, thus lessening harvesters' environmental impact, unlike the caution needed with other forest products. Far from eliminating this plant from its host tree, it is much more likely that cutting will encourage new shoots and, in a few years, crops of increased size.

Many collectors pack mistletoe in boxes and, when sorting through the day's pickings, discard damaged pieces, break some into smaller sprays and tie others together in order to distribute the berries evenly. Only fresh, undamaged mistletoe is salable —leaves and berries must be unbroken and unbruised. As the plant is very fragile when frozen, extra care should be taken during cold weather. Because mistletoe can soon lose its freshness, dealers have it graded, packed in cartons and shipped as quickly as possible.

We have found that it is easy to find markets for mistletoe in large population centers during the Yuletide season. Local florists, Christmas tree sellers, craft shops and boutiques, as well as major processors of forest greens are ready buyers.

We collected mistletoe with a couple on the Washington coast last year who scanned the newspapers for announcements of large gatherings during the Christmas season; they then contacted the people concerned and offered mistletoe to decorate their halls. "We charge $5 for a carton

about the size of a beer case," they told us. "We pick about 10 boxes a day and usually don't have any trouble getting rid of them by selling them in large lots." Small wonder that this pair seemed to reflect more than their share of Christmas cheer! Lacking the time and patience, we never did get around to trying their method, selling instead to a forest greens processing plant in the area. We've known people who set up shop on the nearest street corner to hawk their wares without a street vendor's license (which, if they're obtainable at all, are apt to be quite expensive) and kept their running shoes on and a weather eye open for the gendarmes. This retail method, complicated as well as profitable, risks a whopping fine or worse.

Passing through Grant's Pass,

Oregon last winter, we came across a young fellow selling sprigs of mistletoe in a shopping center for 50 cents apiece. While we were standing nearby, gauging his success (considerable, we thought), his father walked up. "We do this every year," he told us. "The seller's permit costs us $35, but we usually clear about $100 a week for less than 20 hours work, so we feel it's worth it."

Holly

Holly is another traditional Christmas decorative that brings substantial earnings. Large shipments of holly are sent to market each year from natural stands on the Atlantic coast from Maryland to Texas, and from the inland valleys of Tennessee, Kentucky and West Virginia. Some of the best holly comes from the Delmarva Peninsula on the eastern shore of Chesapeake Bay, Maryland, where its gathering just before Christmas has been a favorite activity of rural residents since the late 1880s. Farmers and tenant families of that period found holly harvesting an excellent means of earning extra income once their food crops were marketed in the fall.

Large quantities of Peninsula holly were shipped throughout North America, but most were made into wreaths and sold to local dealers or at the Fruitland, Maryland, holly auction. The depression days of the

American holly (ilex opaca) has spiny, glossy leaves with red berries. This is the most common holly used for Christmas decorations.

1930s were the height of the Peninsula holly industry when over five million wreaths were produced for the Christmas markets.

The holly tree is hardy and has few insect and disease enemies, but it can be ruined by overzealous cutting. Responsible harvesters prune individual trees lightly, using sharp tree trimmers—not axes, saws or corn knives—and make their cuts clean, at junctions of main and lateral branches. Holly, like mistletoe, brings eager buyers at Christmas and can be sold using the same techniques.

Evergreen Boughs

Evergreen boughs, perhaps the most ubiquitous of all Christmas decoratives, come from natural stands and are used in a great variety of ways: for outdoor commercial displays, street decorations, wreaths, door swags, and mantle pieces.

Many kinds of evergreen trees — fir, cedar, hemlock, spruce and pine — can be found in all of North America's forest regions.

Typical of the many prosperous dealers in evergreen boughs is the Meadow Ruh Shop of Clearwater Lake, Wisconsin, which sells about 5,000 cartons of Christmas greens annually. Ten to 15 bough-cutters are used each year to harvest the assortment of boughs of jacks, Norway and white pines, cedar, balsam and spruce which go into each shipment, along with a few loose cones and a bunch of ground pine.

Another of the many popular bough-cutting areas at Christmas time is a coastal stretch 200 miles long and 40 miles wide, which covers southwestern Oregon and extreme northern California, where the Port Orford white cedar, highly regarded for its lacy, gracefully-drooping boughs of lustrous green is found. In the heart of this range of prized trees is the coastal town of Port Orford, from which the cedar gets its name. Many of the town's residents make a good supplementary income from mid-September when the shoots are mature enough to collect, until the following spring, when the new growth appears. Just before Christmas the demand (and the price) rises to a point that incites the greatest number of the community's citizens to roam the forest for these boughs.

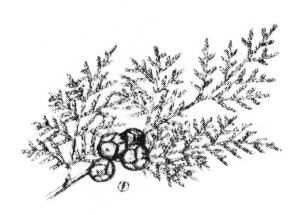

The Port Orford cedar (chamaecyparis lawsoniana) is found in a narrow strip along the Pacific Coast of southern Oregon and northern California. An attractive evergreen; some shoots are tipped with creamy white, others with yellow, golden, or blue-white foliage.

Port Orford cedar is but one of the species of evergreen boughs harvested across the country at Christmas. Firms pay from ten to 15 cents a pound—experienced bough-cutters can harvest from three to four hundred pounds of boughs a day.

To get the boughs out of the bush, harvesters often put them up in bundles of 30 to 40 pounds to pack them from deep in the forest—often miles. The easiest method of collecting boughs is from freshly-felled trees in logging operations. A more difficult but popular technique is for harvesters to climb trees, often with safety ropes and spurs, bend the branches toward them and cut off the ends with a hand pruner, which is the most popular tool for cutting boughs within easy reach. Where the branches are thick and light-weight, long-handled lopping shears are used.

The best quality boughs are often found at the highest reaches of the tree, where they get the most sunlight. For these, collectors sometimes use a long-handled tree trimmer with a rope-operated blade. The handle can be extended from five to 25 feet by adding sections or by using an aluminum telescoping pole.

Growth studies conducted by the Forest Service have shown that removing more than 25 percent of the live crown of a tree during any five year period will shock the tree and retard its development. To prevent this, responsible harvesters are careful not to take too much from any one tree. Another method of insuring future bough production is for harvesters to make their cuts just above a large vigorous branch fork, about three or four feet from the tip of the branch. Within four or five years, both forks will likely develop new, harvestable tips.

Like most forest greens, boughs should be delivered as soon as possible, to prevent them from drying out. Most markets require that boughs be about 24 inches long. Branch tips are considered the best sprays, but laterals of sufficient length are also salable. An extra reason for haste is that the Christmas season is short and hectic, and buyers face deadlines from wreath-makers and other customers.

Fruit-Tramping

The teller's face was incredulous when she looked up from the paycheck I had just given her, awarded for apple-picking by the Brincken's Oasis Orchards of Brewster, Washington. "You must have been picking fruit for several years," she said, her voice full of awe.

"No," I answered, "this is just my second season."

It was apparent that my response failed to alleviate her surprise, but the long line of people behind me discouraged any lengthy explanation, so we both turned our attention to the task of converting $930 into traveler's checks. Later, as I pointed our van southward, back to California after five months of following the harvests, I described the teller's reaction to Marie. She laughed, "I'll bet the poor soul is thinking of giving up her job and hitting the road as a fruit tramp."

The teller, of course, had not realized that the check represented the earnings of two people—for 18 consecutive days, each one consisting of nine hours or more of hard, steady work. Because we saw the job through to the end, we also reaped a $75 bonus, "to help defray travel expenses," said farmer Roland Brincken, one of the most fair-minded orchard owners we have worked for. With these factors taken into account, our check translated out to about $2.50 per man/woman hour—certainly not the kind of wages one ordinarily gets excited about.

However, for those like us, of gypsy blood and not really looking to get rich overnight, the life of a fruit tramp (I use this term in the same spirit as other pickers do) offers more than money. Its basic attraction is that it allows us to reconcile a love for travel with a need to work. Also, we were working outdoors, at our own speed and without a boss breathing down our necks every minute (providing you're careful not to bruise the fruit).

The reason the boss isn't apt to be concerned about an individual's picking pace is that he doesn't have a vested interest in it. What you don't get around to picking, someone else will. Picking fruit is piece work, which means that the harder you work the more you make. Your earnings can be enough to cover travel expenses or — if you're willing to expend the effort — they can build into a nest egg sufficient to see you through a long winter.

The harvest seasons in each region tend to be short, generally, from four to six weeks, so if it's your goal to make a stake that will allow you to loaf through the winter, you have to hustle while you can. Couples naturally fare better financially than those who go it alone.

Last year, we began fruit-picking in Linden, California, in late May, following the cherry harvest from there to Benton City, Washington, and finishing it up at Flathead Lake, Montana, in early August.

From Montana, we drove back to Hood River, Oregon, for the pears. At the end of five months of fruit-harvesting, we had made $3,500 and saved over half of it. We figured travel expenses ate up much of what we earned, but then the opportunity to experience new vistas is worth a lot to us.

Picking fruit is a pleasant way to make money. Especially enjoyable are those moments of peace and contentment when you pause to survey the countryside from atop your ladder and bite into a juicy piece of fruit that tastes like nothing you have ever bought in a store. These moments inspire a sense of discovery. From your "crow's-nest," you gaze over an ocean of fruit trees, stretching for miles in every direction and waving at times under a gentle wind. There's a special pleasure in watching the progress of sun and clouds across the heavens.

The fall apple harvest provides special bonuses in the vivid colors of the fruit trees, and the squadrons of geese arching across the sky, signaling a time of change. What is it in the rhythmic honking of these majestic birds that strikes a responsive chored in so many of us earthbound souls?

It's a mistake to assume that picking fruit is easy. Climbing up and down tall ladders with a picking bag that can weigh up to 30 pounds can leave you with more aching muscles at the end of a day than you thought your body possessed. But they ache less as the season progresses. Remember that many city people pay for the privilege of getting their bodies tuned up, while here the farmer is paying you.

During harvest time most people are engaged in more conventional pursuits, so labor is scarce, making another job you can usually have for the asking. Farmers are usually eager to hire anyone with strength enough to knock on their doors. Beginner or no, it takes little expertise to pluck a piece of fruit. To make the kind of money some oldtimers do takes considerable finesse, but the farmer doesn't expect great performances from everyone he hires—his main concern is that you get the fruit off the tree unbruised; what you earn is more your concern than his.

Owning two hands in reasonably good working order is usually enough to land the job. Farmers usually supply all the necessary equipment, picking containers, ladders, etc. But if you become serious about this line of work, you might find it advantageous to invest a few dollars in your own equipment. This saves you from having to head down the road for less

favorable employ when the owner of a good orchard tells you, "I'm sorry, I'd like to hire you, but I'm out of picking bags." Also, we've found that owning your own picking apparatus impresses farmers with your earnestness.

Second-hand stores in harvest areas are good sources of inexpensive equipment. In these stores, we purchased two apple-picking bags for $5 each in Yakima last year. The year before, in Wenatchee, we picked up a kidney-shaped cherry picking bucket, along with harness, for $2.50. There are few other occupations where the tools of the trade can be had so cheaply.

Like most pursuits, your fruit-picking improves with practice. You learn that there are subtle tricks to getting the fruit off the tree quickly and without bruises. And how you set your ladder can make a big difference. You can learn much from the veterans. It's been our experience that folks who follow the fruit are among the world's most congenial and will eagerly share their know-how with greenhorns.

In fruit-tramp country, you shouldn't be afraid to speak first, if necessary. It's unlikely that you will be answered with the same zombie-like stares you get for trying to be friendly in the city. Some of our most helpful information has come from pleasant conversations with other pickers in laundromats of harvest areas. Even better than the knowledge gained are the friendships formed with kindred spirits.

Some oldtimers call ahead to farmers each year and will be able to tell you when the harvest is due further up the road. They can also advise you on the best and worst places to work. Nevertheless, ask as many questions as you will, some of fruit-tramping's lore comes only with experience. For example, it took us a full season before we learned to distinguish a good orchard from a bad one. The former contains young, assiduously-pruned trees on well-kept and reasonably level land. An orchard lacking any of these attributes will likely pay more per bin/box/bucket, but not enough to compensate for the harder picking.

A good apple orchard, for example, paying $5.50 a bin, will likely earn a reasonably skilled picker from $10 to $15 more by day's end than an orchard of big trees, or one on a side hill, paying $6.50 per bin. That's a big difference.

The best orchards are usually found by driving around looking for them. If you don't want to do this, or get exasperated after an hour or two of fruitless (excuse the pun) searching, you may elect to go to one of the orange farm labor trailers found in agricultural areas at harvest time. These are grower-oriented facilities, but they usually have jobs, even though the trees may require extension ladders and the farmer might be hard to please. Keep in mind that the best-picking orchards seldom need to advertise for help.

If you're new to an area, however, the orange information trailers can be helpful for obtaining information about local crop conditions and getting pointed in the right direction. You haven't got much to lose by trying the job they give you. One of the nice things about fruit-picking is that you are always free to head down the road whenever the situation isn't to your liking.

Although we usually prefer to let our earnings accumulate, farmers will always give you your pay at the end of the day if you ask for it. As a married couple, we often find it convenient to

Symbol for farm labor information.

be paid separately, each using our own social security number. An individual is entitled to earn $150 before having social security deducted; separate checks save the farmer some bookkeeping and you some immediate dollars.

Some fruit regions treat their harvesters better than others. The Yakima Valley is not one of these; not only is the pay consistently lower, but there is little lodging available. Not that this would matter—as most pickers have recreation vehicles or tents—except that most Yakima orchardists, unlike farmers elsewhere, also prohibit pickers to camp in their fields during harvest season. This leaves pickers with two alternatives: the two local campgrounds which are, as a rule, not only jammed but mosquito-ridden; and the area's motels, which raise their rates in honor of the occasion.

For these reasons, most experienced harvesters bypass the Yakima area altogether, leaving the work in that area to the "homeguards" and the increasing numbers of illegal Mexican aliens being brought in each harvest season. The same is true in the Hood River, Oregon, area.

Housing isn't a problem in most harvest areas, however. Many have farm labor camps where you can get room and board for a nominal fee. In places like Brewster, farmers supply their pickers with cabins during the harvest season, at no charge. Some of the cabins aren't much; others, like those provided by Roland Brincken, are as good as most motel lodgings in the area.

Housing is nice when the weather turns nippy during the fall apple harvest, but a roof over the head isn't something that most pickers worry about during the summer months. Then it's enough just to wedge your tent or camper in among the others and make yourself right at home in the orchard of a farmer glad to have you. Two or three weeks in one of these instant communities can be a satisfying experience; you will meet fine people from all over the country.

If there isn't a shower by the orchard where you're camping, you likely won't have to look far for a river or a lake—a little water refreshes both body and soul at the end of a hot summer day. Campgrounds are another possibility when following the fruit, but they often are some distance from the orchards.

Opinion is divided over which is the best fruit to pick. Many consider cherries the best money-maker. Just as many boost apples. Others swear by prunes (without laughing). But I've never heard a good word for pears; they are the heaviest of all fruits and they come off in August, which tends to be a wickedly hot month where they are grown. The combination of weight and heat isn't compensated for by better wages, we've found. That is why some pickers prefer to pass up pears altogether, searching out an area with prunes, peaches or apricots instead.

Apples are our personal picking favorite, one reason being the cooler fall weather. Also, we seem to be more consistent picking apples. Marie and I average from eight to 10 bins a day together—a feat that is by no means earth-shaking; some oldtimers pick this much working alone. It usually takes about 25 full picking bags to make a bin, for which you're generally paid from $5.50 to $6.50.

Cherries are our second favorite, mainly because they are not so physically demanding. Because there's so little weight to carry, children can do very well picking them too. Wesley, our 12-year-old, had no trouble making over $10 a day as a cherry picker last summer. Before he went back to school in the fall, he had earned enough for a new fishing rod and reel, a set of school duds and his own savings account to draw on through the winter. He had fun besides, with the excitement of travel and plenty of youngsters his own age in many of the orchards. Like us, he enjoyed being left to work at his own pace. Not surprisingly, he often chose a nearby swimming hole or a good fishing spot over more cherry-picking—particularly after two weeks' work and the accumulation of a sum he felt would last him the rest of his life. Not all orchards are open to children, by the way, as the insurance policies carried by farmers sometimes don't cover them.

Cherry-picking may not appeal to those who like to sleep late. Mid-day temperatures can be scorching indeed; therefore, most pickers attack the trees at dawn in order to beat the heat. By early afternoon—when the thermometer may read between 105 and 110 degrees—harvesters are off sitting under a cool shade tree boasting about who got started the earliest.

Wesley's idea of summer vacation means, for one thing, sleeping until 9 or 10, but Marie and I usually managed to get onto our ladders by 5 a.m. Even so, we were often awakened earlier by the rapid "thump, thump, thump" of cherries hitting the bucket of some "high-roller" who must have been sitting on his ladder when the first rays of morning sunlight revealed

the small, round outlines of the fruit.

"High-roller," you might be curious to know, is fruit tramp terminology. An oldtimer told us, with only a little tongue-in-cheek, that it refers to "anyone who can pick as much as he claims he can."

Despite their early start in the mornings, most cherry pickers still get plenty of sleep, as they usually go to bed at dark. And take it from us, you always sleep soundly after a day of orchard work.

The main disadvantage of cherries is their vulnerability to the weather. A hard rainstorm after a particularly hot spell will cause not only the cherries to split, but you too.

Of course, most times, if you're rained out you need only head up the road and wait for the next crop to come in. But not if you have driven from Washington to Flathead Lake, Montana—this is the end of the line for the cherry-picking season in the West. Since the Montana cherry crop is often wiped out by rain, many harvesters refuse to make the long trek there each year.

Most of those who do travel to Montana to pick cherries in July value the natural beauty of this unspoiled region more than making much money. If they meet expenses and have a good time, they consider the trip a success.

The cherry orchards of Flathead Lake ring the edge of this great body of water. For pickers, this means some great vistas to enjoy from ladder tops, and only a short trip after a hard day's work to a cool dip in the clear waters. The fishing is also excellent in Flathead Lake, and in many surrounding lakes and streams.

Flathead Lake is not the only harvest area in the West that offers both natural beauty and a variety of recreational pleasures. Lake Chelan and Wenatchee are other favorites of ours. Next year, when we travel east to participate in North Carolina's long apple harvest, we'll surely find more nature-blessed picking regions.

Fruit-tramping is an ideal way to subsidize a summer vacation. It can give every family member the satisfaction of contributing to the cause, and you're assured of unique experiences at every turn—and aren't they the ones that bring the lasting memories?

There are fruit and vegetables waiting to be picked all over this land. If you want to know precisely what, where and when, there are useful government publications you can send for. One is the booklet "Crops Requiring Seasonal Hired Workers," available for $1.25 from the Superintendent of Documents, U.S. Government Printing Office, Washington, D.C. 20402. You can leaf through this publication and perhaps find an area you would like to visit that has something to harvest at a suitable time.

Another publication we have found very helpful is "A Guide to Seasonal Farm Work Areas in the Far

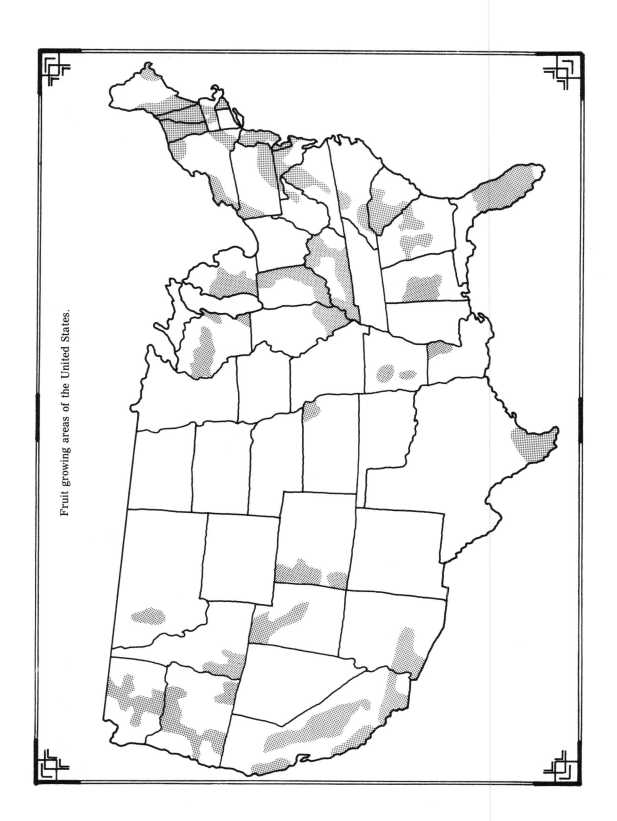

Fruit growing areas of the United States.

APPROXIMATE HARVEST DATES

MAJOR FRUIT—GROWING AREAS	apples	cherries	peaches	pears	citrus
Alabama			Jun 10-Jul 20		
Arizona					continuous
Arkansas			Jun 15-Aug 15		
California	Jul 15-Oct 30	May 15-Jul 1	May 15-Oct 15	Jul 1-Sep 30	continuous
Colorado	Sep 30-Nov 5	Jun 25-Jul 30	Aug 13-Sep 17		
Delaware	Jul 5-Jul 30		Jul 25-Aug 25		
Florida					continuous
Georgia			Jun 1-Aug 8		
Idaho	Sep 17-Nov 15				
Illinois	Jun 20-Sep 31		Jul 10-Sep 5		
Indiana	Jul 1-Sep 31				
Kansas	Jul 1-Sep 30				
Kentucky	Aug 25-Oct 15		Aug 3-Sep 15		
Louisiana	Jun 15-Jul 15				
Maine	Aug 16-Oct 31				
Maryland	Aug 1-Nov 15		Jul 10-Sep 15		
Massachusetts	Aug 20-Oct 25				
Michigan	Aug 1-Nov 15	Jun 30-Aug 15	Aug 5-Sep 25	Aug 1-Oct 25	
Montana		Jun 15-Aug 15			
New Hampshire	Sep 15-Oct 15				
New Jersey	Jul 15-Nov 15		Jul 15-Sep 15		
New York	Aug 1-Nov 15	Jun 15-Aug 15			
North Carolina	Aug 1-Nov 1		Aug 1-Aug 31		
Oregon	Sep 8-Nov 5	Jun 8-Jul 20	Aug 8-Sep 20	Aug 15-Sep 30	
Pennsylvania	Aug 15-Nov 30	Jul 4-Jul 31	Jul 31-Sep 30		
Rhode Island	Sep 20-Oct 20				
South Carolina			May 16-Aug 31		
Texas					continuous
Utah	Sep 20-Oct 31	Jun 25-Aug 10	Aug 20-Sep 20	Aug 20-Sep 20	
Vermont	Sep 14-Oct 25				
Virginia	Jul 31-Nov 30	Jun 1-Jun 31	Jul 15-Aug 31		
Washington	Sep 5-Nov 1	Jun 20-Aug 1	Aug 1-Sep 15	Aug 15-Sep 20	
West Virginia	Aug 5-Nov 5	Jun 15-Aug 15			
Wisconsin	Aug 16-Nov 1				

Western States," an information-packed brochure available free from the Government Printing Office. There are similar publications for other regions of the country. These give crop areas, seasonal work periods, information centers, local offices of the State Employment Service, farm labor offices and farm labor camps.

If you already have your itinerary planned for the summer, but are still interested in picking up a few travel-expense dollars in a satisfying way, keep your eyes open for those bright orange trailers while you're driving through the countryside. If you find one, drop in and ask what's doing. Chances are they'll be glad to tell you.

You can pick fruit pretty well year-round, by the way. When the Washington apple harvest finished up last October, many pickers headed for California, Arizona and Florida to harvest citrus fruit during the winter months.

Those who have been fruit-tramping for some time establish a set route for themselves, returning to the same farmers year after year—the ones who treat them right. Not orchard owners like the one we worked for one hot July day in Selah, Washington. He pulled us out of the row we had been working on to pick a big, snarly tree near an old outbuilding and a pile of scrap lumber. We had noticed the people picking it earlier retreating across the orchard, picking

bags slung over their backs. "I wonder why they're quitting so early?" I had asked Marie.

My answer came as I was setting my ladder up at the base of the monster tree. It came in the form of an angry buzz near my feet. The back of my neck developed a tingling sensation and I froze for what seemed to be an interminable period of time before backing up—slowly. Marie had just brought her ladder over to the tree and stopped dead in her tracks seeing the expression on my face. "What's the matter?"

I picked a couple of cherries out of the bucket strapped to my waist and threw them into the grass where I had just been. Again there was a staccato clicking. "I think we just quit," I said. "I think we did," Marie agreed.

The farmer was indignant when we suggested that we could find safer places to work than his orchard. "No rattlesnakes around here," he scoffed. His disclaimer didn't get the backing of other pickers we talked to that evening in Yakima's Sportsman's State Park. "The hills up there are crawling with them," a grizzled oldtimer told us. "Never catch me working up there."

The best advice I can give, should you elect to sample the life of a fruit tramp, is to stay away from mean snakes and mean farmers. There are picking jobs where you don't have to contend with either one.

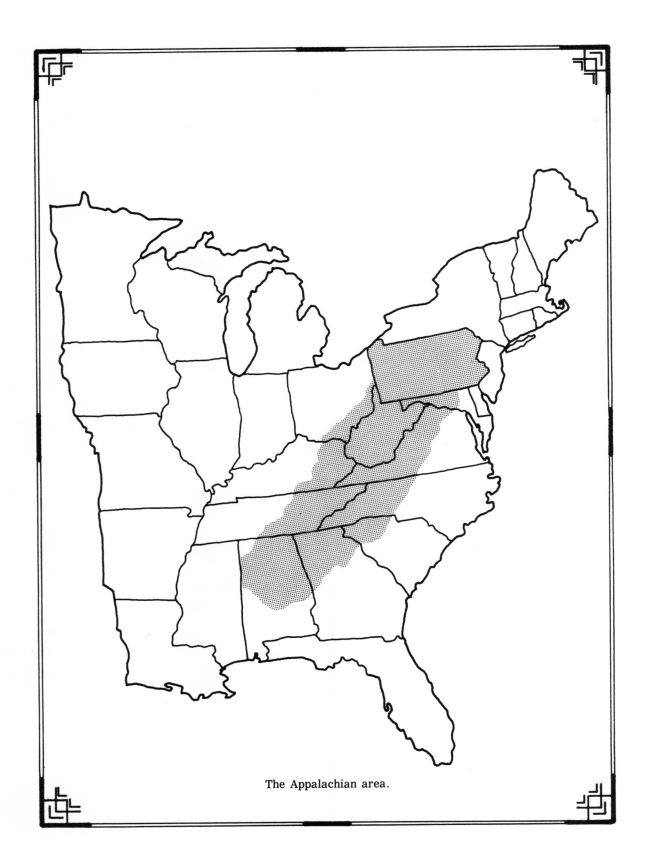

The Appalachian area.

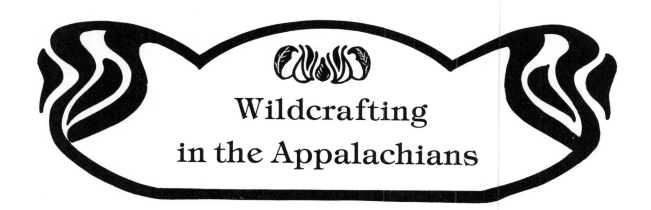

Wildcrafting
in the Appalachians

Ginseng, goldenseal, May apple, foxglove, snake root, witch hazel, black haw, lobelia—the names alone are enough to stir one's spirit. These are just a few of the marketable herbs growing wild in the Appalachian Mountains and other forested regions of the eastern United States and Canada. The demand for leaves, roots, and barks with medicinal properties is historically high and promises to get higher. "In the next five years, I look for a big increase in natural-product medicines," predicts Dr. Norman A. Farnsworth, professor of pharmacognosy at the University of Illinois. "The time is ripe partly because of rising public interest in natural foods and environment. But newly discovered sources of crude drugs and better extraction methods are also factors. Our vegetable and animal kingdoms have hardly been touched . . ."

The future of wildcrafting (the Appalachian term for wild herb gathering) seems assured. Fifty percent of modern drugs depend upon medicinal plants. "Appalachian dealers buy and sell more than 125 species of medicinal plants," writes Arnold Krochmal of the U.S. Forest Service in Raleigh, North Carolina. A botanical-economist, his job is to expand use of forest resources and, at the same time, help mountain people supplement skimpy incomes by harvesting nature's bounty. A stroll through the woods becomes keener if you're hunting "green gold." There are few forested regions in North America that don't offer a marketable herb or two. The richest areas are in the mountain regions of the eastern U.S. and Canada.

Wildcrafting is one of the world's oldest vocations. Despite many years of persistent harvesting, even the Appalachians still contain vast stretches of largely untapped sources of crude drugs. Some important medicines are derived from them. From the dried leaves of the foxglove plant comes digitalis, the world's leading heart stimulant and regulator. Snake root is prized as a valuable aid in the treatment of high blood pressure and emotional disturbances. May apple is the basis for a drug produced in Switzerland to treat brain and lymphoid tumors. From witch hazel comes an effective lotion for treating insect bites.

Ginseng

Most valuable of all crude drug plants, as far as collectors are concerned, is ginseng (panax quinquefolium). It is a distinctively-shaped plant which takes five to eight years to mature; it grows 8 to 15 inches high and usually bears two to five prongs off a main stem, each having five leaves (two of them smaller than the others) which resemble those of a strawberry plant.

Ginseng can be found in the rich, moist soil of well-drained hardwood forests ranging from the southern part of eastern Canada through the eastern United States as far south as Georgia and Alabama and as far west as Minnesota. Ginseng is often referred to as "sang" by Appalachian collectors, who receive from $60 to $70 for each pound of dry roots.

So far, attempts to cultivate ginseng have had limited success. It's a temperamental plant which seems to grow best under natural conditions. Domestication is further discouraged by the fact that cultivated varieties are not valued as highly for their medicinal effects and dealers will pay only half of what they pay for the wild product.

Though hunters of wild ginseng today must range further afield in search of this curative herb than their predecessors, they still managed to earn about $4 million last year.

Some health food stores in this country carry tonics containing ginseng, but most of the roots (over 100,000 pounds last year) are shipped to markets in the Orient where the plant has been integral to the Chinese materia medica since Confucius praised its powers over 2,000 years ago.

Although ginseng is also native to Asia, the American variety has found a ready market in the Far East since its discovery on this continent in 1717 by a Jesuit priest, Father Joseph Francis Lafiteau, in the woods near Montreal. Lafiteau had been alerted to ginseng's possible existence in North America by a fellow clergyman serving in the Orient, who had written "if it is to be found in any other country in the world, it may be particularly in Canada, where the forests and mountains very much resemble those here."

Ginseng is not yet esteemed for its medical properties by the health establishment of the western world, although considerable research is underway which could soon dissipate such skepticism. The Soviet Union, particularly, has studied ginseng and is enough impressed with its virtues to put several hundred acres under cultivation.

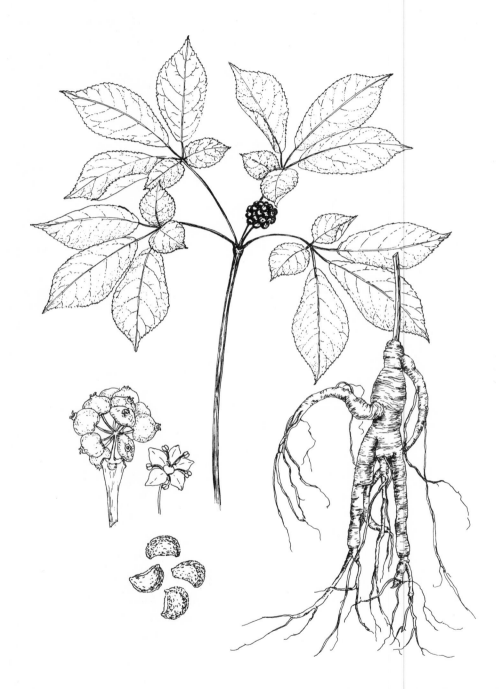

Branch, root, flower, berries, and seeds of American ginseng (panax quinquefolius). Grows to about one foot tall. Leaves of mature plants consist of five leaflets. Flowers are greenish yellow, borne in clusters. Fruit is a bright crimson berry, containing one to three wrinkled seeds the size of small peas. The mature root is spindle-shaped, two to four inches long, and up to one inch thick.

Ginseng's name derives from two Chinese words: shen-seng, which translated means "man-plant." This is explained by the fact that a ginseng root sometimes forks into "legs" at the bottom and arm-like roots near the top which gives it a crude human likeness. This configuration makes the root even more valuable to Orientals as an amulet. Legend has it that a Chinese emperor once paid $10,000 for such a root. Even today, wealthy Orientals are said to pay $200 to $500 for a ginseng root of human form.

Aside from its occasional use as a good-luck piece, it's primarily as a panacea (a term that is thought to have originated from the plant's generic name) and an aphrodisiac that ginseng continues to be so highly valued by Asian peoples. A most potent treatment according to the "Atherva Veda," the ancient medical book of India: "This herb will make thee so full of lusty strength that thou shalt, when thou art excited, exhale heat as a thing on fire."

The early settlers of the midwest found ginseng a powerful antidote for what ailed them. For them, the wild plant spelled the difference between success and failure after a series of natural disasters—unusually severe winters, locust plagues and crop failures—was followed by the panic and depression of 1857. As a result, settlers who had borrowed heavily to carve their homes out of the wilderness were unable to make good on their loans.

These pioneers were ready to call it quits when traders arrived from the east and acquainted them with the commercial value of ginseng, a plant which flourished in the forest areas around the settlements. The news sparked a "green gold rush." Whole communities took to the woods in search of "sang" and it wasn't long before the frontier economy took on new life, thanks to a generous transfusion of dollars from the ginseng trade.

A.R. Harding, an early buyer of furs and medicinal herbs, wrote of the early heyday of ginseng digging: ". . . sometimes as high as one hundred pounds of root would be secured from one such plot. Women as well as men and boys hunt the root. The plant is well known to all mountain lads and lasses and few are the mountain cabins that have no ginseng in them waiting for market."

The China trade was also fed by trappers and hunters, who were always one step ahead of the settlers in the push west, earning their living by selling furs and medicinal herbs. Indians, too, dug the valuable garantequen, trading it for kettles, blankets, guns and other goods.

When a collection of ginseng root was sufficiently dried, it could usually be sold in a nearby village, often to the same person who bought furs, hides and other forest products. Collectors in out-of-the-way places awaited the arrival of buyers from the east, who traveled through the frontier country with a string of pack horses—from Indian village to trapper shack to immigrant farm house—purchasing furs and roots from the people.

The heavy trade in ginseng in the eastern mountain regions was noted as early as 1784 by George Washington, who wrote: "In passing over the mountains, I met a number of persons and pack horses going in with ginseng."

The ginseng business was still healthy many years later when a buyer who traveled through Ohio, West Virginia, Kentucky and Pennsylvania wrote of his surprise at finding 21 sugar barrels full of ginseng roots—about 3,000 pounds in all—waiting for him at a fur dealer's in Portsmouth, Ohio. In 1841 alone, American merchants shipped 640,000 pounds of the roots to China from New York and Philadelphia.

Understandably, the intensity of ginseng harvesting eventually made the plant extremely scarce near settled areas. Then, as new industries came to the foothills, insuring steady employment and economic stability, the appeal of ginseng hunting lessened; entire generations grew up almost oblivious to its cash-earning potential. As a result, ginseng escaped extinction. It even seems to have made a comeback. Plant aficionados, Euell Gibbons among them, claim there is probably more wild ginseng in America today than there was 50 years ago.

It appears that the collecting of wild medicinal plants will remain a viable means of earning money for years to come, especially for the mountain folk of the eastern United States during summer and fall when the ginseng ripens.

A day spent gathering medical botanicals usually brings collectors from $20 to $40. Yet there are days when hunters find a good patch of sang and take home as much as $100 for their labors.

Trucks have replaced pack horses these days, but eager buyers still make trips up tortuous roads to pick up leaves, roots and barks at rustic mountain homes. "On a real fine haul, we've carried about nine tons," claims Ralph Proffit, who collects for the Wilcox Drug Company, founded in 1865 by the great-grandfather of the present owners, Kenneth and Gary Wilcox.

During his stops, Proffit exchanges small talk with mountain wildcrafters while he weighs their big burlap sacks of dried vegetation on his portable scales. Then he throws the sacks onto his truck, writes a check and drives down the road to the next pick-up. Proffit's route also includes mountain stores, where he often picks up neighborhood collections of 1,500 pounds or more. Last year, the crude drug buyer wrote out checks totaling more than $50,000 to one country store in Virginia.

What are the prices paid for the different botanicals? They vary considerably, according to the price list of the L.S. Dinkelspiel Company of Louisville, Kentucky, which quotes these per-pound rates for some of the most sought-after crude drug products:

L.S. Dinkelspiel Co.

INCORPORATED

229 EAST MARKET STREET

DEALERS IN
WOOL
FURS, HIDES
GINSENG
GOLDEN SEAL
FEATHERS
ETC.

TELEPHONE 585-2731

LOUISVILLE, KY. 40202

ESTABLISHED 1856

June 1975

SHIP YOUR GINSENG - GOLDEN SEAL - MAYAPPLE
BLOOD ROOT - WAHOO AND OTHER ROOTS
TO DINKELSPIEL IN LOUISVILLE FOR 119 YEARS

Dear Friend:

Try and get us the roots we have listed below and ship often to us. We assure you of paying the full market prices and giving you fair and honest weights, also prompt payment upon arrival of your goods. "You will like doing business with us."

We are paying today the following prices delivered here for clean and dry roots and barks: (Prices subject to change without notice.)

ROOTS	Per lb.	ROOTS	Per lb.
WILD GINSENG	$53.00 - $55.00	Virginia Snake Root	$16.00
Golden Seal Root	2.50	Senega Snake Root	2.00
Golden Seal Tops (leaves)	1.25	Black Haw Bark of Root	.40
Mayapple Root	.25	Wild Ginger Root	.75
Blood Root	.80	Dark Lady Slipper	1.25
White Slippery Elm Bark	.35	Star Root	.35
Wahoo Bark of Root	2.50	Star Grass	1.50
Wahoo Bark of Tree	.80	Twin Leaf	.35
Beth Root	.35		

(Other roots, full market value)

Ship all Ginseng and Golden Seal via parcel post whenever possible. Mayapple and other roots, in lots of 100# or more, it would be cheaper to ship via truck. Small lots, ship parcel post.

Also interested in purchasing wool, beef hides and raw furs (in season.)

CHECKS MAILED THE SAME DAY YOUR SHIPMENTS ARE RECEIVED.

Yours very truly,

DEL BYRON

Other Medicinal Plants

Although other medicinal plants are priced much lower than ginseng, they tend to be more common, which means that they can be just as profitable to the collector. You won't get rich collecting these natural products, but it does afford a good excuse, if you need one, for a stroll in the woods. Like the early settlers of the midwest, and many Appalachian mountaineers today, you might even find wildcrafting a good way to meet the payments on your homestead.

If you do take up wildcrafting with any sincerity, you would be wise to heed the words of Mary Call, plant collecting heroine of the movie Where the Lilies Bloom: "Wildcrafting is a sight easier to read about than do . . . It is not an occupation for the squeamish or for those who like to lie abed mornings or for anyone with weak feet or unwilling legs."

Whatever your degree of enthusiasm, if you want to try your hand at collecting wild plants for the drug industry, you first must know if there are any marketable herbs in the vicinity. Here, as with beginning any forest vocation, the first step is to check with the nearest branch of the Forest Service. There you can learn most everything you need to know and also, if you intend to harvest in areas under forest service jurisdiction, pick up the necessary permits.

If there's no buyer of medicinal plants in your vicinity, you should write to dealers and request their price lists. From them you can learn which botanicals are in current demand (most lists include at least 20) and choose a buyer whose terms are most attractive.

The surest way to become a successful collector of crude drugs is to dog the footsteps of someone experienced. If you have to go it alone, you should obtain a good plant reference. Your local library probably has several useful publications. Two to look for are "Recognizing Flowering Wild Plants" by William C. Grimm ($7.95 from Stackpole Co., Cameron and Kelker Streets, Harrisburg, Pa 17105) and "The Herb Book" by John Lust ($2.50 from Benedict Lust Publications, 490 Easy Street, Simi Valley, Ca 93065).

No matter how carefully you study your plant guides, you may have difficulty distinguishing the various species. For example, many low-growing plants (Virginia creepers among them) have leaf clusters similar to those of ginseng.

Therefore, before filling your sacks with wild plants, you would be wise to dig a few samples of the species you intend to collect and send them to your prospective buyer for verification. If they are what you thought they were, start digging. The only equipment you need is a shovel or mattock for digging, and a few sacks.

Veteran wildcrafters are careful to protect the forest environment—

as much out of respect for their vocation as for nature itself. Adhering to a few common-sense practices assures a future crop as well.

No matter what natural products you're collecting, leaves, roots, or bark, you can follow certain procedures that encourage replenishment. When collecting leaves, resist the temptation to completely strip the tree or shrub. Instead of harvesting an entire bed of plants, leave a few to reproduce themselves.

When gathering ginseng plants — which take five to eight years to produce a saleable root — wildcrafters take care to dig up only the more mature plants; generally, those with three or more branches off the main stem. Uproot ginseng with great care. If the root turns out to be less than four inches long and hence of negligible value, replant it tenderly in the original spot.

Another advantage of digging only older plants is that they often have small supplementary roots, which exist to maintain the plant in event of damage to the main root; these may be replanted after the larger root is removed.

Many wildcrafters won't dig roots during the summer growing season. At this time of year, the roots are deficient in medicinal properties and also lose more weight during the drying process than they do at maturity in the fall. Also, by waiting until autumn to dig, ginseng hunters will find ripe berries on the plants.

Smart collectors replant these berries in the same location, thereby insuring another crop in a few years. Some wildcrafters take a few of these berries home to plant in the backyard. Cultivating ginseng is a good way of earning extra income, but it is a slow process and considerable care has to be taken to duplicate the natural habitat. Ginseng grows best in loam soil, like that in the hardwood forests of the north. Partial shade is also important and can be furnished either by trees in your backyard, or by a lath shed.

If you're interested in growing ginseng, write for a handy booklet by the Dept. of Agriculture, "Growing Ginseng" (Farmers Bulletin No. 2201) — sending ten cents to the Superintendent of Documents, U.S. Government Printing Office, Washington, D.C. 20402. The techniques of ginseng cultivation are also well-described in A.R. Harding's "Ginseng and Other Medicinal Plants" — a $4 paperback issued by Emporium Publications, P.O. Box 207, Boston, Mass 02129.

The proper preparation of botanicals is extremely important, otherwise the collector risks having them rejected by the dealer. All stock must be clear of foreign matter; roots should be rinsed in clean water — but never leaves, stems or flowers.

When peeling such barks as wahoo and black haw, take care to remove their woody parts. In the case of coarser barks (elm, hemlock,

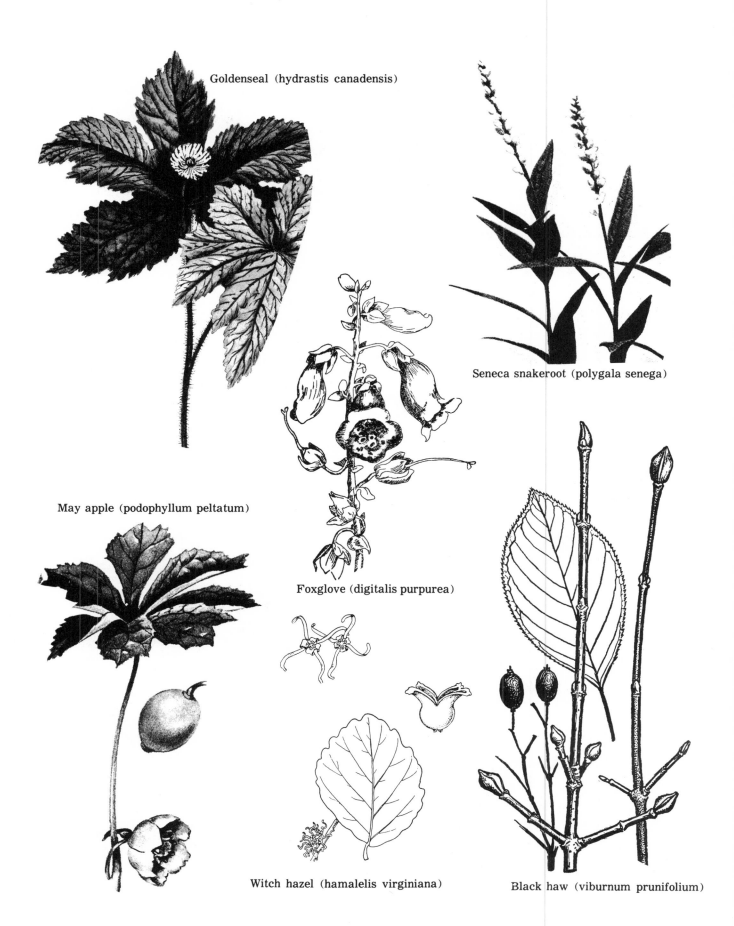

Goldenseal (hydrastis canadensis)

Seneca snakeroot (polygala senega)

May apple (podophyllum peltatum)

Foxglove (digitalis purpurea)

Witch hazel (hamalelis virginiana)

Black haw (viburnum prunifolium)

poplar, oak, pine and wild cherry), the outer layer should be shaved off before the bark is removed from the tree, a process known as "rossing."

All products must be thoroughly dried. This is done by spreading them out thinly on clean surfaces and exposing them to light and air. To insure getting premium prices—given for those plant materials that retain their rich natural colors—direct sunlight and moisture should be avoided during the drying process.

To make sure that crude drugs are prepared to the satisfaction of the buyer, send him a sample of your collection before forwarding the complete lot. Once acceptance is guaranteed, pack the lot in burlap bags or sturdy boxes and ship by Parcel Post; this is the cheapest way, unless you have large quantities, then send by a trucker.

This done, all you have to do is sit back and wait for your check, which most dealers remit the same day shipments are received.

Buyers: Most of the following firms will be pleased to hear from you—if you're serious about collecting botanicals, and not merely indulging an idle curiosity. (Enclose a stamped, self-addressed envelope with all inquiries.) This list is by no means complete, but it does include many major buyers.

S.S. Belcher and Co.
P.O. Box 148
Princeton
West Virginia 24740

Smoky Mountain Drug Co.
935 Shelby St.
Bristol
Tennessee 36720

L.S. Dinkelspiel Co.
229 E. Market St.
Louisville
Kentucky 40202

F.C. Taylor Fur Co.
227 E. Market St.
Louisville
Kentucky 40202

The Frank LeMaster Co.
P.O. Box 192
Londonberry
Ohio 45647

Wilcox Drug Co.
P.O. Box 391
Boone
North Carolina 28607

St. Louis Commission Co.
4157 N. Kings Highway
St. Louis
Missouri 63115

William J. Boehner and Co.
259 West 30th St.
New York, N.Y. 10001

Consolidated Fur and Ginseng Co.
157 West 29th St.
New York, N.Y. 10001

Hensely Fur Company
Box 153
Waynesville
Missouri 65583

United Fur Brokers
258 West 29th St.
New York, N.Y. 10001

Q.C. Plott Fur and Ginseng Co.
4062 Peachtree Road
Atlanta
Georgia 30319

S.B. Penick and Co.
100 Church St.
New York, N.Y. 10007

Herbarium Inc.
P.O. Box 620
Kenosha
Wisconsin 53140

Coeburn Produce Co.
Second and Grand Streets
Coeburn
Virginia 24230

Peeling Cascara Bark
in the Pacific Northwest

A few years ago, during a drive along the Oregon coast, we stopped at a feed store on the outskirts of Coos Bay, a picturesque lumbering port. As we approached the entrance, we noticed a message posted in the window—"We Buy Cascara Bark."

Our curiosity aroused, we asked the elderly clerk to explain. "It's a pleasant way of earning a few extra dollars in the summer months," he told us. "Peeling cascara bark is pretty popular with folks hereabouts . . . the activity has financed hot rods for more than a few of Coos Bay's young bucks."

A woman standing next to us at the counter nodded agreement. "Yes, and it's also kept a few families eating during strikes and other troubled times."

She seemed eager to discuss the merits of peeling cascara bark. "I go out every chance I get during peeling season," she added. "I average about $20 a day . . . but I sure enjoy puttering around in the woods on a nice day as much as I do the money to be made—some people work a lot harder at it than I do and, of course, earn much more."

We spent the next two days in Coos Bay, getting some car trouble tended to, and noticed several more businesses with signs soliciting cascara bark. One was a large packing plant just off the main street, operated by I.P. Callison and Sons, Inc., who are also buyers for a variety of other minor forest products found in the Pacific Northwest.

During those two days, we asked more questions of cascara peelers we met. And we came across many—few residents of this forest-oriented community hadn't tried peeling cascara bark at least once.

Extracts from cascara bark—also known as chittim bark, we were told—have been used as a safe and effective laxative for many generations. The bark's medicinal benefits were known to the Indians, who passed along their knowledge to the Spanish missionaries of Old California.

The Spanish priests named the bark cascara sagrada, meaning "holy bark," believing it was the same chittim wood used in the construction of Noah's Ark and King Solomon's Temple. The missionaries were mistaken; rhamnus purshiana, as the tree is botanically known, is unique to the western part of North America, although other species of the buckthorn family are found in Europe and Asia.

The missionaries weren't the only early visitors to take note of the cascara tree. Members of the Lewis and Clark expedition noticed it lining the shores of the Columbia River in 1805. In 1816, Escholtz, the Russian botanist, wrote of the tree's existence on the California coast.

Not until 1877, however, when Dr. J.H. Bundy of Colusa, California, published an account of the bark's medicinal value, did it become well-known. Soon after Bundy's report, Parke-Davis presented a legitimate concoction to the medical profession, and a new industry was born in the Pacific Northwest.

Although the commercial range of the tree extends into northern California and southern British Columbia, most of the bark—over three million pounds last year—is harvested in the coastal regions of Oregon and Washington. While a small amount of the yearly total is taken from plantations, most of the crude drug comes from natural stands.

The collecting of cascara bark has a short season; it varies according to location and elevation, but generally runs from the end of April to late August. Because the sap is most active at this time of year, the bark peels off with relative ease under the proddings of a knife or spud.

Unfortunately, rain is common in the Pacific Northwest during the spring months, which brings discomfort to those who tramp the forests, and also tends to blacken and stain the bark, lowering its value. Drying—an essential operation before offering to buyers—is difficult during rainy spells. Peelers of cascara bark are therefore most active in the Northwest woodlands during the sunny days of June, July and August.

Under ideal conditions, good peelers can collect 200 to 500 pounds of wet bark in a day. About 50 percent of this weight is lost during drying.

The market price of dried cascara bark has fluctuated greatly in the past, from a low of six cents a pound in 1940 to a high of 32 cents in 1947. Presently, the price for a pound of dried cascara bark is hovering between 25 and 30 cents. "Green" bark brings about one-third the price paid for dried bark.

Experienced peelers can make $40 on a good day. Rank amateurs should expect no trouble making at least $10, pretty good "pin money" in these tight times—particularly if you're one of those who have trouble regarding a day spent in the quiet woods as "work."

Cascara trees are generally small and tend to be overlooked by the timber industry. The mature cascara reaches 20 to 40 feet high, with a diameter of 6 to 15 inches. Exceptional trees have been found, however. Imagine the joy experienced by the peeler in the Skagit River region of Puget Sound, who harvested a record 1,000 pounds of bark from a tree 60 feet high and three feet in diameter. His yell probably matched the 49'ers who struck the Mother Lode!

Due to the popularity of cascara peeling in the Pacific Northwest, you have to probe deep into the forest to find such a virgin tree nowadays. Instead of spending an entire day looking for a monster tree, you'll probably do better with smaller trees with easier access.

Deforested areas—150,000 acres are created annually in Oregon and Washington—are especially good sources of cascara bark, thanks to birds and bears who feed on the dark blue cascara berries and then scatter the seeds. The cascara tree is an eager grower.

You can estimate the amount of bark a tree will yield by measuring its diameter. Generally, these corresponding amounts will be collected: 3-inch diameter, 5 pounds; 5-inch diameter, 10 pounds; 7-inch diameter, 15 pounds; 10-inch diameter,

35 pounds; 12-inch diameter, 50 pounds; 17-inch diameter, 122 pounds.

The bark of the cascara tree, like most gifts of nature, requires careful harvesting procedures to insure its preservation. In issuing permits to bark peelers, the Forest Service demands that all trees be felled before peeling them, leaving a stump of 6 to 12 inches with a sloping surface to shed rain and retard decay. This stump should not be peeled, so that it may send out new sprouts, from which another crop can be harvested in a few years.

Conscientious harvesters assure maximum harvest by peeling only the older trees and removing the bark from all branches down to a diameter of about one inch. By adhering to these practices, cascara-peelers assure us of a continuous supply of bark to fill an important medical need.

To get the best price, remove moss and lichens which often spot the bark's surface. These growths can be removed before the tree is cut down by rubbing the trunks and limbs with a gunnysack or by scraping with the peeling tool.

The bark is peeled from the tree in sheets about two feet in length by various types of knives or spuds. The peeler first cuts around the circumference of the trunk and limbs at points two feet apart, and then makes one longitudinal slash from one cut to the other. The bark slips off rather easily during those months when the

sap is most active.

The best way to dry cascara bark is in the sun, spreading it out on a canvas or platform with the inner sides placed face down. Four to seven days is usually enough for drying. Care should be taken to cover the bark during the night if there is a possibility of heavy dew or rain.

In the rainy climate of the Pacific Northwest, sunshine may not be available for long periods. A warm room is often used for drying. Extreme temperatures are to be avoided; under no circumstances is the bark dried in an oven or near a hot stove. Nor should green bark be piled in a heap and allowed to mildew. Peelings that are improperly dried or handled under unsanitary conditions may be rejected by the buyer.

To test for complete dryness, try breaking a piece; if the bark snaps cleanly, it is considered done. Also, you can tell properly dried bark by its clear-orange or golden-yellow color, indicative of a high percentage of chemical content.

When dry, bark is cleaned of foreign matter and broken into small pieces. These are then packed into ordinary burlap sacks, which hold from 50 to 75 pounds. Dried bark is easy to break up and does not deteriorate with age (if it is kept dry) —the beauty of this is that if the price drops before you can get your bark to market, you can store it until the price is more to your liking.

As one major buyer explains: "We do not arbitrarily set the price we pay for bark. The current prices vary from time to time, and this is determined by world market conditions of supply and demand and not by our firm."

You usually don't have to look far to find a buyer of cascara bark in the Pacific Northwest; even the most unpopulated areas usually have one nearby. In the larger towns, in addition to feed stores and other businesses eager to buy cascara bark, there's usually a branch packing plant of one of the "big three" of cascara bark trade—Pacific Coast Cascara Bark Company, I.P. Callison and Sons Inc., and the Western Crude Drug Division of the S.B. Penick Company. These three account for the lion's share of the bark sold by west coast firms to pharmaceutical houses.

In almost every region where cascara bark is peeled, there is a story of a first-timer who drove eagerly up to a dealer's with a vehicle full of bark, expecting instant fortune and getting instead a lesson in botany and a huge dose of disappointment which comes with barking up the wrong tree (pun intended). Frequent errors are made by inexperienced collectors who mistake red alder, willow, dogwood and hazel for the chittim tree. There are ways to protect yourself from such a faux pas. As with most pursuits involving the harvesting of forest products, it's good to have someone experienced show you the ropes.

You can always resort to books—a good way to gain a grasp of most subjects. A field guide I've found pretty handy during my forest meanderings is "Trees of North America" by C. Frank Brockman, which comes in a $3.95 pocket edition issued by Golden Press (Western Publishing Co.), 850 Third Avenue, New York, N.Y. 10022. The color illustrations, unlike those of similar books, are accurate; with the aid of this volume, you should have little trouble picking out a cascara tree from imposters in the forest. Another good reference is "Western Forest Trees" by James Berthold Berry, available for $3 from Dover Publications, Inc., 180 Varick St., New York, N.Y. 10014.

You can always resort to books—a good way to gain a grasp of most subjects. A field guid I've found pretty handy during my forest meanderings is Trees of North America by C. Frank Brockman, which comes in a $3.95 pocket edition issued by Golden Press (Western Publishing Co.), 850 Third Avenue, New York, N.Y. 10022. The color illustrations, unlike those of similar books, are accurate; with the aid of this volume, you should have little trouble picking out a cascara tree from imposters in the forest. Another good reference is Western Forest Trees by James Berthold Berry, available for $3 from Dover Publications, Inc., 180 Varick St., New York, N.Y. 10014.

Actually, a cascara tree is not difficult to identify. The bark is usually a brownish hue, although a thin growth of lichens on the bark's surface may give it a grayish color. The leaves of mature cascara are distinctive; although they resemble red alder, they are a darker green and more oblong in shape; also, the perimeter of cascara leaves are finely toothed, while the alders have blunt-toothed edges.

The cascara produces black, fleshy berries which are found in clusters of two or three in the axils of the leaves. Each berry contains two or three seeds, which can be sold to nurseries. Forestry officials can direct you to seed buyers. Other characteristics of the cascara tree are the yellow color of the freshly-cut bark and its extremely bitter taste; chew on a piece of cascara bark and you'll have a sour taste in your mouth for days.

Experienced collectors look for the best specimens on fertile, well-watered lands. Good places are in Douglas fir forests, along river bottoms, the borders of streams and on flats and ridges in the foothills.

Other Medicinal Plants and Trees

Besides cascara bark, there are a few other medically-useful plants and trees in the Pacific Northwest, although the demand is intermittent and their future somewhat uncertain.

Among them is the tree-growing quinine conk, purchased by crude drug firms for European markets. These conks (of the quinine fungus fomes laricis), also native to several European regions, are used to produce agaric acid, a medicinal chemical.

Quinine conks don't grow in profusion and are hard to find. They are usually found growing on snags, windfalls and decadent old-growth Douglas fir, ponderosa pine, sugar pine and western larch. Favorite picking spots are in old burns and logging operations in decadent old-growth timber.

Quinine conks are identified by their cylindrical, hoof-like shape and annual growth layers on the underside —with age, these become quite elongated, chalky and crumbly. Conks will attain a weight of 50 pounds or more, which, at 50 cents a pound, means quite a bonanza for those loggers and other forest habitues who occasionally stumble across them.

Prince's pine (chimaphilia umbellata) is another plant valued commercially for its medicinal properties. A low-growing, evergreen herb common to many forest areas of the Pacific Northwest, particularly southwestern Oregon, the whole plant (roots, stems and leaves) is dug up by collectors and dried for sale to crude drug dealers. Destined for multiple use as a tonic, astringent and diuretic, the plant brings about 50 cents a pound.

Used in the treatment of jaundice, Oregon grape roots are also purchased occasionally by crude drug firms in the Pacific Northwest. During buying periods, the dried roots of both the tall Oregon grape (mahonia aquifolium) and the short Oregon grape (mahonia nervosa) are salable, bringing about 25 cents a pound.

That's about it for the medically-useful plants in the West. The Pacific Northwest does not boast nearly as many crude drugs as the eastern mountain regions, but it's sufficiently blessed to provide many people with what they consider to be a convenient and enjoyable means of earning a few dollars, especially during the summer when the peeling is easy.

Buyers: Further information concerning the gathering of cascara bark and other crude drugs can be obtained from the following firms, the west coast's major buyers. (Be sure to enclose a stamped, self-addressed envelope with your queries.) Addresses are for the main offices of these companies; all have buying stations liberally sprinkled throughout the coastal regions of the Pacific Northwest where cascara bark is harvested.

Callison and Sons Inc.
Lloyd Building
Seattle, Washington 98101

Pacific Coast Cascara Bark Co.
520 N.W. 23rd Ave.
Portland, Oregon 97210

S.B. Penick Co.
Western Crude Drug Division
1000 W. 8th St.
Vancouver, Washington 98660

Northwestern Drug Co.
1815 East D
Tacoma, Washington 98421

Collecting Seed Cones

"Weyerhaeuser paying cash for Douglas fir cones, $7 per sack. Inquire Dick Howard, Libby area, Coos Bay, 267-6494."
—classified advertisement taken from the Coos Bay newspaper "The World"

It may come as a surprise to learn that gathering seed cones during fall months is no longer practiced by squirrels alone. People too are getting into the act.

Like the squirrel preparing for winter, mankind is driven to prowl the woodlands of the nation in search of cones. Our forests are becoming rapidly depleted and there is a growing awareness of the urgent need to restock cut-over lands. Consequently the forest seed business, still comparatively young, is growing steadily.

According to the Forest Service, "the future for cone-collecting looks good. Forest landowners are demanding greater quantities of seed each year for reforestation . . . it seems that a strong demand for forest tree seed will continue for many years." Considerable amounts of seed cones are purchased by timber companies. For example, Weyerhaeuser, one of the largest private forest land ownerships in the world (5.6 million acres) plans to plant from 85 million to 135 million trees during this decade. Seed cones are also sought by state forestry departments, the Forest Service and private nurseries. And there is a constant, heavy demand from European and South American countries for their own reforestation programs.

Because of this ready market, thousands of pounds of seed cones are harvested annually from wild stands, and the public is depended upon to collect much of it. The rewards are ample, including the inner satisfaction of participating in a valuable conservation program as well as the remuneration—upwards of 20 dollars a day.

Although more than 600 species of woody plants—almost every type of forest tree in America—are deemed valuable for conservation planting, about 130 species comprise the bulk of the seed trade. Some 25 varieties, mostly conifers, account for most of the total area planted and seeded. The tree most prized for its seed is the Douglas fir, its cones being collected in great quantities in the Pacific Northwest from about mid-August (at low elevations) to the end of October (at high elevations).

The best seed harvesting time for each tree species varies from season to season and place to place. By learning the seed ripening times of each tree in your area, it's possible to turn your outdoor excursions into treasure hunts that will pay nice dividends.

The first step is to find a cone-buyer. He can supply the necessary permits and tell you everything you need to know—which species are in demand, best areas and elevations for picking, ripeness and seed count requirements, and labeling instructions. Certain procedures are required by the seed certification program. Weyerhaeuser Company foresters are especially accommodating to cone collectors. They often supply not only instructions, but also maps, sacks and permission to pick on company property.

Locating a cone-buyer is relatively easy. You can usually find one by inquiring at the offices of local

foresters and county extension agents. Some buyers solicit help by placing classified ads in newspapers in forest areas. Often, timber companies and commercial seed firms use local stores in cone-collecting regions as buying stations—they usually carry posters in their windows proclaiming "We Buy Cones."

Before embarking on a seed cone hunt, collectors are advised to negotiate a minimum purchase price with the buyer. Cone prices are dependent upon several factors, one being the species; the large noble fir cone will bring $1.50 to $3 per bushel, while the very small western hemlock cone earns $5 to $14 a bushel.

The exact amount paid collectors also depends upon cone quality and crop year conditions. The former is usually determined by seed content. This is learned by splitting the green cones longitudinally with a sharp knife or a mechanical cone-cutter which has a hinged blade similar to a paper cutter. Buyers test several cones taken at random from each sack before accepting the lot. You can insure that yours will meet the approval of buyers by occasionally checking them yourself in the field and taking pains to collect only those of good quality. Douglas fir cones that "cut" four, five or six seeds are most valuable, while those that contain only one or two seeds are worth little.

The value of cones may also be reduced by worm damage. (You can generally spot a wormy cone without cutting it open—indicators are boring holes, globs of pitch and cone disfigurement.) And there's no use collecting open or partially-opened cones that have dried out and lost their seed to the wind.

Most conifers only produce a heavy cone crop every three to five years. During intervening seasons, the crop may be medium, light or even a complete failure. Therefore, seed is usually purchased in sufficient quantities during good seasons to last through the lean periods. There is usually work for cone collectors each year, however, because a bad season for one tree species may be a good one for another. Even for the same species, quality can vary greatly in different zones.

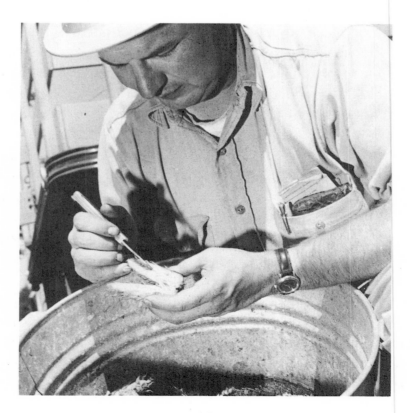

For the beginner, the most popular method of cone collection is to try to outwit the squirrels; that is, to try to find where they store their winter supplies. They cut cones from trees as soon as fall weather begins and continue until the weather becomes too severe or until the cones are over-ripe and lose their seed. Squirrels are discriminating collectors —they select only the best seed cones, so stumbling onto one of their caches is a lucky break indeed. The size of individual squirrel collections may be as much as 10 or 15 bushels.

What does a squirrel cache look like? You can be sure it will be well-camouflaged, covered with leaves and brush. It will likely be in a moist place —often near a stream—for the squirrel knows that if the cones become dry they will open and the seed pop out. Good places to look for cone caches include damp tree hollows, and burrows under fallen trees and rocks. Shredded cone remains on old stumps will tell you if the area you're hunting in is favored by squirrels.

Because Mr. Squirrel is just as conscious of the soaring crime rate as the rest of us, he takes great pains to hide his bounty. As a result, the cone harvester can spend days scouring the woods and never find a squirrel hoard. You needn't fear that a squirrel will face starvation come winter as a result; each squirrel has several cleverly hidden caches containing far more food than he's likely to need during the cold months.

Harvesting from trees felled during logging operations ranks with squirrel-robbing as an easy method of collecting cones. But take care to gather only from trees logged after their seeds have matured.

Most cones are harvested from standing trees, the best being those that are young, healthy and well-formed. These are usually from 30 to 60 feet high and heavily laden with cones. Open-grown trees of this sort normally have several branches near the ground, which makes climbing relatively simple; older trees, as well as younger ones growing in dense stands, often lack lower branches and are more difficult and hazardous to climb. A few cones on standing trees may be picked from the ground, but most of the crop is found in the middle and upper parts of the tree. While not mandatory, special equipment makes cone-collecting from standing trees more efficient. Standard household items can often be adapted to fit the needs of cone-pickers.

Ladders can sometimes be helpful, but they are cumbersome and not suited to rough ground or to areas where cone-bearing trees are located some distance apart. Pruning hooks or similar tools are good for cutting cones from branches, but they should not be used to cut the branches themselves—such mutilation of the tree can retard its growth. Climbing spurs are popular with some harvesters, but they should be used only

for scaling large trees as younger ones with thin bark can be badly damaged by spurs. Use of a climbing belt that loops around the tree trunk insures safety and frees both hands for speedy picking. Do-it-yourselfers can easily assemble their own safety belts out of 5/8 inch manila rope and some buckles. Caution: climbing ropes should not be used on young trees, as a running rope can cut deep grooves into tender bark, these may girdle the tree and kill the top as a result.

Collecting high in a tree with a gunny sack often means groping for its opening with each handful of cones. We found that an apple-picking sack hung from straps around the shoulders eliminates this problem. A common house pail tied to the belt also works well.

Because a collection of cones soon becomes quite heavy, some harvesters carry several sacks up a tree with them; when their pickings become heavy, they just put them in a sack, tie the top closed and drop it to the ground. Many collectors find a pole with a hook at the end helpful for reaching the tips of branches, where most cones are located.

The most common method of cone-picking is for harvesters to climb to the top of the tree, secure a belt around it, and place both feet firmly on two branches where they join the trunk. Since branches pull up easily, they work from the top down. Employing this method, they clean most trees of their cones by working only three positions on the tree.

There are certain safety practices to remember: climbing should only be done by people who don't fear heights; footing should only be sought on live branches—dead ones are treacherous; most important, always collect with another person who can help in the event of an accident.

Last year, we saw pickers in the Cascades using homemade, long-handled rakes to strip cones from branches up to 30 feet high. Although a bit unwieldy, requiring frequent rests, it's an excellent tool for families—youngsters can pick from the ground while their father brandishes the rake.

What kind of picking can you expect as a cone harvester? According to the Forest Service, "an average Douglas fir seed tree may produce about two bushels of cones which can be gathered in about two hours by an experienced picker."

Seed cones are usually delivered to buyers in two-bushel burlap sacks. Since sacks that are bunched up and tied at the top will not usually hold two bushels, the best way to secure a full cone sack is to tie two corner ears about four inches long, like sacks of potatoes or grain.

Sacks must then be labeled with tags supplied by the cone buyer. Facts that must be recorded on these include the general area and elevation where the cones were collected so that their seeds may be planted under similar conditions.

Once sacked, seed cones will quickly heat and mold, so most harvesters try to get them to a buying station the same day they are picked. If cones must be stored, it should be in a cool, well-ventilated location with each sack upright and separated from the others to permit air circulation.

If the buyer finds the collector's cones acceptable, he pays cash on the spot. If quality or quantity are questionable, adjustments are made in the prices. Local buying stations deliver the cones to processing plants where they are dried in a kiln to open them. The seeds are then removed in a shaking machine. Weyerhaeuser's plant processes 500 bushels of cones a day.

Each year, in late fall and winter,

many of the seeds are sprayed on logged-over land from helicopters. Some seeds are saved and planted in nurseries. When they grow into seedlings they are transplanted on rough, brush-covered areas.

It's estimated that 20 new forest giants will hatch from each Douglas fir cone collected—a fact which the cone harvester can take considerable pride in.

The district offices of governmental agencies like the Bureau of Land Management, the U.S. Forest Service and state foresters are good sources of information for those interested in collecting seed cones. So are the following commercial seed firms, many of which operate buying stations in cone-producing areas. Those who write and ask what they are in the market for, are advised to include a stamped, self-addressed envelope with their inquiries.

FOREST SEED DEALERS:
E.C. Moran, 1st and 1st N, Stanford, Montana 59479
Herbst Brothers, 92 Warren St., N.Y., N.Y. 10007
Mount Arbor Nurseries, Shenandoah, Iowa 51601
Plumfield Nurseries, 2105 N. Nye Ave., Fremont, Nebraska 68025
Henry Field Seed Co., 407 Sycamore St., Shenandoah, Iowa 51601
Boyd Nursery Co., Highway 55, McMinnville, Tennessee 37110
Marshal Nurseries, N 2nd St., Arlington, Nebraska 68002
Brown Seed Co., P.O. Box 1792, Vancouver, Washington 98663
Conifer Seed Inc., 5182 Sunnyside Rd., Salem, Oregon 97302
Esses Seed Co., 401 S 7th St., Montesano, Washington 98563
Garrison Seed Co., 103 S.E. 3rd, Milton-Freewater, Oregon 97862
Pacific Forest Seeds, P.O. Box 1363, Medford, Oregon 97501
Silvaseed Co., P.O. Box 118, Roy, Washington 98580
Simpson Timber Co., P.O. Box 308, Albany, Oregon 97321
Weyerhaeuser Co., Box B, Tacoma, Washington 98401

Worm-Grunting, Pollen-Collecting, Moss-Gathering

"Rummp, rummp, rummp." The sounds, similar to those from a herd of grunting pigs, vie with the first sleepy cries of the forest's bird life. Startled, a gray squirrel looks up from a heap of maple leaves he's been rummaging through in search for breakfast. Motionless, like a pointer, he stares at the kneeling figure of a man in worn denim coveralls, barely discernible in the cold gray light just before the sun rises. The "rummping" sound comes from him as he steadily rubs a metal bar back and forth across the top of a wooden stake driven into the ground.

A strange pastime at an unusual time of day, most observers would agree — except those who are one of the thousands of "grunters" who earn all or part of their income in this manner in the forests of the South each spring and summer.

Fellow grunters realize that making like a fiddler on an imbedded stake does more than arouse a squirrel's curiosity. Most important, they've learned, is that it creates vibrations in the ground for several feet around the stake — throbbings that drive earthworms to the surface, where they are gathered and put into two-quart cans or "kegs."

The worms are later sold to wholesale distributors, who supply bait shops in several southern states. Anglers who eventually decorate their hooks with the bait probably don't have any more fun catching fish than the grunters did gathering the worms.

Bait harvesters are seen in greatest numbers in the woodlands of the Florida panhandle, particularly the Apalachicola Forest, where grunting ranks grow to a full-size army during "the season" — from April to October. (Worms spend the winter months below the frost line, forming huge companionable balls with hundreds of their fellow creatures; this prevents the evaporation of moisture from their skins.)

"The area in and around the Apalachicola National Forest is some of the best 'gruntin' grounds' anywhere," says Bris Price of the U.S. Forest Service in Tallahassee. The cacaphony of enthusiastic grunting which fills the Apalachicola Forest during summer months was enough to pull CBS News' Charles Kuralt off the road a couple of years ago. It was with trepidation that the roving correspondent made his way through the Florida bush toward the commotion, duty-bound to bring new phenomena to the attention of viewers across the land, yet fearful of being rooted to death by a herd of wild boars.

We surmise that Kuralt was both relieved and amazed to discover not wild pigs, but people engaged in one of this country's more peculiar occupations. It was news even to him that the damp woodlands of the South were a source of virtually inexhaustible and easy-to-get natural riches— long and wiggly, but valuable nevertheless.

Close by the Apalachicola National Forest is Blountstown, considered the center of Florida's million-dollar worm-grunting industry. Blountstown covets the title of "Worm Capital of the World," but the appellation is grudgingly denied by the citizenry of nearby Sopchoppy, who feel that its worm-hunters are the gruntiest.

What can't be argued, however, is that in spite of all the back-bending, grunting is fun. But you're right when you surmise that not everyone who gets out of bed to grunt before sunup can be doing it for laughs. The added incentive is the wages; the going rate is $9 to $10 for each can of 500 worms, but the price varies with the time of year, dipping to $6 and $7 when school lets out in summer, allowing entire families to head for the woods in search of worms.

Since good grunters can collect eight to ten quarts of wigglers each time out, the pay is pretty good, especially when you consider the short work day. Any grunting heard after 10 a.m. is gratuitous since earthworms have a greater aversion to the sun's rays (which can shrivel them), than to pulsating environs.

In order to time their needs with the earthworms', entire families— mom, dad, and toddlers barely big enough to grab one of the slithery critters—can be found in the forests of the South in the dim morning hours, in the flickering light of kerosene lamps.

After some hours of grunting, the bait harvesters of the Apalachicola Forest return home and prepare their catch for sale to the distributors— there are several in the nearby towns of Sopchoppy and Blountstown. Worms are counted stored in quart containers filled with damp sawdust. If they have been taken from black soil, the sawdust soon cleans them off, restoring their bright red color.

Grunts are sometimes heard even after the worms are delivered to the

distributors. These are grunts of disgust from the buyers caused by the earthworm's inability to survive overly long hauls. Vibrations not only lure the worms to capture, but if prolonged, will also do them in. Therefore, the distributors confine their sales area to nearby states.

Grunting is another outdoor occupation blessed by low overhead. The only equipment needed is a wooden stake about 18 inches long (wild persimmon or oak works best, experts say), known as a "stob" in grunter's jargon. The steel strip used by grunters to drive the stob into the ground and then to "play the tune" is called a "roop iron." An auto springleaf serves nicely. And last, you will need a tomato can to hold the captured worms.

Despite the simplicity of the equipment, it's wrong to suppose that grunting doesn't have its finer points. As a bass fiddler needs just the right touch to get a "rise" out of his audience, so does the grunter. "It takes a good man on that stob," according to Arch Porter, considered one of the best grunters in the Apalachicola Forest. "If you vibrate too much, you'll kill the worms. And if you don't vibrate enough, they won't come up." Vibrating "just enough" often brings 100 or more earthworms squirming to the surface near the stake.

Although even experienced grunters are often fooled when trying to evaluate wormy terrain, there are certain tell-tale signs. River banks and other damp spots are considered good worming country. So are areas blessed with patches of "cut grass," a sharp-edged forest weed sharp enough to cut one's hand. Also look for thread-like trails left by wigglers on the earth.

Many experienced bait harvesters claim that earthworms can be found in streaks wherever the mineral content of the soil is to their liking. Often, worm-hunters will mark out the perimeters of such a streak before they go to work, in the belief that it's a waste of time to grunt outside this area.

The best grunting of all comes right after an area has been burned over. Then it's easy to spot worms as they come to the surface lured by southern pied pipers. Cooperatively, the government occasionally permits grunters to burn grass and brush off forest lands.

It's not surprising that unexpected blazes, and the appearance of hordes of grunters on the scene before the embers have cooled, have sometimes generated epidemics of paranoia amongst southern landowners. Consequently, there have been some efforts to have grunting banned in the South. But such strivings have come to nought; reason being, perhaps, that grunting is an endeavor that involves many segments of the community—even private landowners, many of whom lease out grunting rights on their property, for rates ranging from five to twelve cents per hundred worms harvested.

You may agree that there's enough for everybody when you consider that 50,000 earthworms will populate an acre of moist ground; several million is not rare. Most sites can be harvested several times a season; some grounds are crawling with fish bait within a week of good grunting, while others can be profitably harvested only two or three times a season.

Although there are few creatures lower on the evolutionary scale than the earthworm, there are surely some who feel that relentless harvesting will soon earn it a place on the endangered species list. Such fears are groundless, due to the earthworm's fantastic breeding capacity. Grunting is one of the few outdoor occupations that conscientious harvesters can pursue without causing ecological damage.

Pollen Collecting

Granted, the gathering of earthworms may seem peculiar to some, but it is not the only one smacking of peculiarity. There is also pollen collecting.

Pollen is used by drug companies in the preparation of tests for certain allergies. Among the pollens most in demand are ragweeds, sages, magwort, elm, box elder, maple, ash, cocklebur, pigweed and Russian thistle. Some veterans of the fruit trail told us that they meet expenses in the spring by collecting pollen in fruit orchards.

Pollen collecting requires day-before preparation; by tying several blooming heads together with string, harvesters mark the best plants and reduce the potential for losing pollen to the wind. Understandably, still days are best for gathering pollen. The same plant can be collected from for several days, until the pollen begins to turn dark.

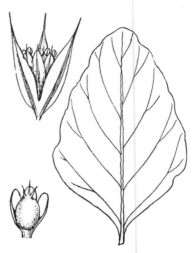

Pigweed (amaranthus retroflexus) is a weed with stout, branching stems, and rough, light green leaves. Flowers are green, in densely compact spikes.

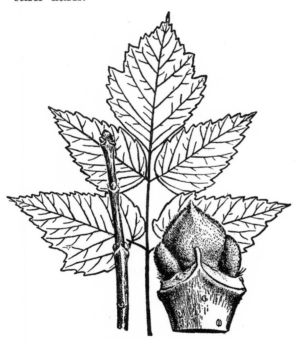

Box elder (acer negundo)

The usual collection method entails rolling the heads of petals gently over a cloth, spreading the blooms carefully with the fingers to release the pollen. After the pollen is harvested, it must be spread out — to a depth of one-quarter inch — on clean,

Russian thistle (cirsium family) has stout stems two to four feet high, which are leafy to the flowering branches, and covered with a soft, whitish wool. A fluffy, silky plume, with white pollen, is sweet-scented but guarded by the numerous prickles.

81

dry wrapping paper (a flattened grocery bag will suffice) in a warm, draft-free room. Then the pollen should be left to air-dry for about four days—if it is not sufficiently dried, molding may occur and cause its rejection by dealers. When dry, pollen is strained through fresh nylon or organdy and stored in clean, dry, screw-top jars or durable plastic bags.

Pollen buyers inspect shipments with a microscope and reject any with impure materials. Thus, pollen should not be collected from plants that have been treated with pesticides; nor should different pollen varieties be mixed together.

Moss Gathering

Moss is another forest crop you may never have considered marketable But it is, and not as difficult to collect as pollen. Good money can be made harvesting moss, which grows in heavy mats or layers on trunks and limbs of trees throughout the land in moist and shady areas.

Much in demand by wholesale florists and other buyers who value both its decorative and water-retaining characteristics, moss has many uses. It is employed commercially in the construction of hanging floral baskets and philodendron columns, as a surface mulch in greenhouses, as a packing material in fish worm containers, as a medium for seed germination and for packing seedlings and other plants for shipment, to list only a few of its uses. Also valued is the peat-like backing of the older moss, which consists mainly of old moss roots and the decayed vegetation that has fallen from surrounding trees or been blown in by the wind.

Moss and backing must be submitted separately to buyers, but collectors are paid the same price for each; in recent years, this has ranged between 15 and 20 cents a pound, dry-weight. Since a good picker working under reasonable conditions can harvest 300 to 500 pounds a day, the money-earning potential of gathering moss is considerable.

During a visit to the Oregon coast a few years ago, we met a moss collector for an evergreen company who cheerfully informed us that he had little trouble making close to $2,000 in this manner each year, working just two days a week. This amounts to about $20 a day, we figured—no fortune, but certainly enough to warrant a hike into the woods.

Although moss can be collected year-round, most buyers prefer to purchase it in its dry state for many reasons, including easier shipping. Collectors have the choice of drying it or waiting until summer when it's least likely to be wet.

Many forest harvesters of the Pacific Northwest find moss gathering a convenient fill-in occupation during those months when the "green treasures" they collect nine months of the year, salal, huckleberry and sword ferns, are sprouting new growth. Last summer these collectors gathered about 40,000 pounds of moss in western Washington and about 20,000 pounds in western Oregon.

Experienced harvesters look for moss at low elevations where annual precipitation is heavy. The best material is often found along creek beds where there is plenty of moisture and shade. It's not unusual to find moss for a stretch of two or three miles along the banks of a stream before, for reasons no one can quite fathom, it runs out.

Easily stripped from the trees, moss is usually carried from the woods in large burlap bags and stored in well-ventilated areas until sold to buyers. When thoroughly dry, the moss is compressed into bales, using uncomplicated devices that can be made for about $5—directions for making these can be obtained from buyers.

As only clean moss is valued, that which grows on logs and along the ground (and, therefore, always full of dirt) is ignored by collectors. So is moss found near coniferous trees, whose needles fall into the moss and are difficult to remove.

Coniferous Needles

Speaking of needles, those of pine, spruce and fir also rank among the forest's potpourri of marketable products; their fragrance is useful in the creation of specialty items like balsam pillows. While the market is limited, their collection provides more than pin money for many people living near resorts where such pillows are sold as souvenirs and gifts.

In the mountain industries of the south, pine needles are also used along with raffia and other weaving materials in the creation of baskets and other small, handwoven articles and novelties. Pine cones are also in demand as a souvenir item in many forest resorts.

In summation, there is an incredible variety of minor forest products whose collection provides income for country people. Granted, such occupational pursuits are both unique and unheralded, accounting perhaps for the strange responses from the uninitiated.

For example, an acquaintance, when told that harvesters of earthworms have been known to earn as much as $100 a day, just grunted. Whether this was an expression of skepticism or in preparation for a trip to the Florida panhandle, I couldn't tell.

Harvesting Wild Edibles

The untamed spaces of North America, though not quite as beneficent as in the earlier days of Indians and pioneer settlers, are still an important source of wild food. For various reasons, modern agriculture has declined to place some wild edibles under cultivation.

It may come as a surprise to learn that the gathering of these edibles appeals to many besides Euell Gibbons. The stalking of wild delicacies has much to recommend it. A day spent in the outdoors is reward enough in itself for many, of course. And the contributions to one's pantry can't be ignored in these days of spiraling food costs. What's more, wild food gathering can often be profitable, as well as enjoyable. Millions of pounds of wild edibles are harvested for market each year by country people seeking extra income.

Berries

Among the most valuable of the wild foods is the blackberry. In Oregon and Washington alone, according to the U.S. Forest Service, "hundreds of tons are picked commercially each year . . . and sold to canneries, frozen food plants and wineries." The wild blackberry, like most fruits, can be made into a variety of confections, including jams, jellies, wines, cordials, pies and cobblers.

Wild blackberries grow in almost all parts of the U.S. and Canada; the best patches grow in sandy, well-drained areas. Wherever they grow, they are delicious and command a good price in the marketplace.

Another ubiquitous wild fruit that invites eager buyers each summer is the huckleberry—or blueberry, as it is called in the East where large amounts are harvested every year (mostly in the northern and New England states, but also in the middle Atlantic, Appalachian and southern regions).

Wherever it grows, the ripening of huckleberry in late summer brings pickers out in droves. The Forest Service reports more than 150,000 visitor-days each year for the 2,500 acre Twin Buttes huckleberry field near Trout Lake, Washington. Many years, its berry yield reaches 250,000 gallons, valued over $1 million.

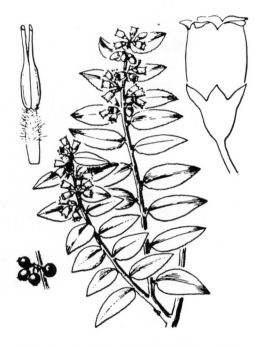

Evergreen huckleberry (vaccinium ovatum)

When you consider that several more millions are earned each year by Pacific Northwesterners who harvest the sprays of the evergreen huckleberry plant for the florist trade, it's obvious that this bush has considerable economic importance.

Of course, the huckleberry was harvested long before the appearance of the white man. The Yakima and Klickitat Indians used to camp in the Twin Buttes region to pick their winter's supply of huckleberries, which they dried and pounded into pemmican or added to venison stew to lend it an exotic flavor. In recognition of the Indians' first claim to the productive huckleberry patches in this area, certain parts have been set aside for their exclusive use.

While Twin Buttes is probably the best-known and most bountiful of the Pacific Northwest's huckleberry regions, it is not the only one. Several hundred tons are also taken from the Puget Sound area each year. Altogether, the Forest Service estimates there are 160,000 acres of wild huckleberry land in Washington and Oregon.

Last year huckleberry pickers in the Northwest were paid $5 per gallon and most experienced little difficulty harvesting five or more gallons a day. Some fruit tramps chose to spend the month of August picking huckleberries on the sun-bathed slopes of Mount Adams rather than participate in the Hood River pear harvest. "The money's just as good and the work's not as hard," one veteran told us.

The best huckleberry patches are usually found on cut-off land, old burns and in forests of second-growth timber. Most huckleberry fields owe their existence to the uncontrolled wildfires that were common before modern fire control techniques were applied. Without fire or other radical disturbance, huckleberry plants are eventually crowded out by trees and brush. The Twin Buttes field, for example, once contained 8,000 acres of an old burn, perpetuated by occasional fires set by the Indians. However, fires have been kept out of the region for over 40 years and the huckleberry area has shrunk drastically. In other parts of the country, huckleberry fields are protected by controlled burning.

Huckleberries, which often grow in tight little clusters near the tips of branches and are sometimes hidden by shiny oval-shaped leaves, can be harvested a variety of ways. Some people pick them one at a time, or by shaking the clusters over a cupped hand, dislodging the ripe berries.

Commercial pickers sometimes use more efficient methods; one is the Indian practice of spreading blankets beneath the bush, then shaking or beating the foliage. A variation is to shake the branches over a large washtub strapped to the shoulders.

This rough treatment won't harm the hardy huckleberry bush, but it will see a lot of leaves collected along with the berries—large processors separate these in a fan mill.

A more common way to pick huckleberries is to carry a small plastic pail, the bail looped through the belt; this leaves both hands free to pick. A bleach jug makes a good container for youngsters—simply cut off the upper portion and attach a string bail. You also might want to take along a large bucket or dishpan; picking containers can be emptied into these.

Although blackberries and huckleberries are the most popular of the marketable wild fruits, there are several others, including raspberries, cranberries, wild grapes, mulberries, and thimbleberries. There are few areas of the North American countryside that don't offer one or

more wild fruits of commercial importance.

No matter what the wild berry, there are usually ready markets for it—frozen food plants, canneries, wineries, as well as roadside stands, local stores (particularly those dealing in organic produce) and private parties. Many buyers solicit wild fruit in the classified sections of local newspapers during appropriate seasons.

Harvesters can make things easier for the buyers by picking directly into plastic berry baskets. This minimizes bruising and mashing. These baskets, as well as empty berry flats, can often be had for the asking from local produce stores. A few years ago, a buyer permitted us to use his wholesale number to buy 12-ounce berry baskets for a penny apiece from a wholesale supplier.

Before embarking on a berry picking expedition, be sure to wear old clothes—berry bushes are often thorny and hard on cloth and skin. Wear long-sleeved shirts and old cotton gloves with the fingers cut out. A brimmed hat to ward off the sun's rays, often merciless during berry picking season, completes the berry picker's ensemble.

An incredible amount of wild fruit grows along public rights-of-ways and can be harvested without needing permission from property owners.

Nuts

"Millions of pounds of edible nuts are sold each year from the forests and woodlands of the nation," reports the Forest Service. The eastern half of the U.S. is particularly rich in nut bearing trees.

One of the most important forest crops is the black walnut. The prices paid add extra zest each fall to family nutting expeditions in eastern Tennessee, Kentucky, southwest Virginia, Missouri and Arkansas. In these regions, the gathering and cracking of black walnuts has long been a popular rural home industry, although state food and drug laws demanding pasteurization have practically eliminated the cracking process.

John E. Wylie, assistant state forester for Missouri, reports "black walnut gathering is a profitable and enjoyable occupation here in Missouri and in most places within the walnut range." Portable walnut hullers owned by major processing companies are assigned to all buying locations throughout the countryside of Missouri and most states that have a significant walnut crop; the gatherer brings in the green walnuts in the hull. The buyer hulls the walnuts free and pays on the basis of the hulled weight.

Last year, collectors were paid $5 for each 100 pounds of hulled walnuts. According to Wylie, the daily earnings of harvesters are "deter-

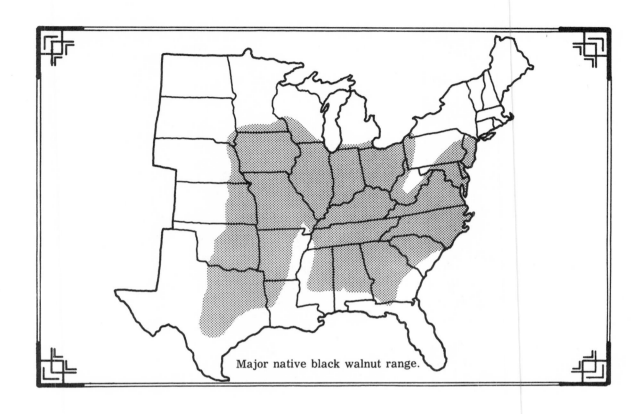

Major native black walnut range.

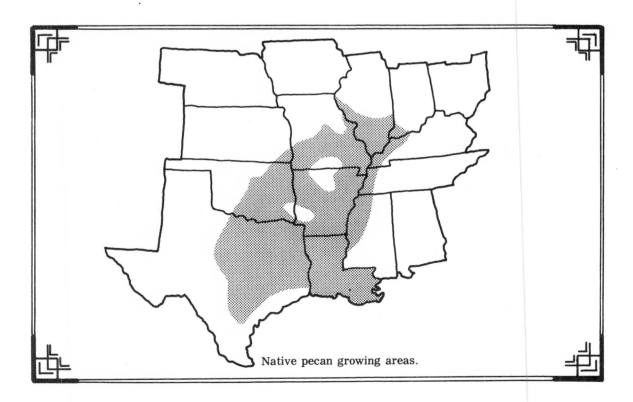

Native pecan growing areas.

mined by the season and the number of trees . . . an individual can collect 800 to 900 pounds a day without too much difficulty in a good stand with a good season."

Missouri boasts the largest black walnut processing plant in the world, the Hammons Products Company in Stockton. They buy from 15 to 25 million pounds of hulled walnuts annually. Another large plant is located in Gravette, Arkansas.

Black walnuts have a variety of commercial uses. Some can be found on supermarket shelves in vacuum-sealed cans and cellophane packages, but the largest part of the wild crop is used to flavor bakery goods, candy and ice cream. The high nutritive

value of the black walnut also makes it a great favorite with backpackers.

Despite their food value, black walnuts were first utilized for their shells, not their kernels. The dense, hard shells make several useful products, including a fine activated carbon used in gas mask filters, a drilling mud used in the oilfields, abrasives to polish castings and automatic transmissions, and extenders for plastics.

Gathering black walnuts is uncomplicated. The only necessary piece of equipment is a burlap bag to hold them. A wild black walnut tree is likely to be quite large, from 70 to 100 feet tall and two or three feet in diameter. A mature tree can produce

200 to 400 pounds of unshelled nuts each year. Black walnut trees like rich soil and are often found in abandoned farm areas and along fence rows.

Other nutritious wild nuts that provide profitable gathering are those of the piñon pine which, according to the Department of Agriculture "are the only nuts produced by an American coniferous tree that have ever had any importance as an article of food or commerce."

harvested in semi-arid regions of New Mexico and northern Arizona, although the piñon pine also grows in Wyoming, Colorado, Texas, Nevada, California and Baja California. Some are marketed in the areas where they are harvested, but most are sent to New York City, where they are bought by transplanted Russians and Italians who "pine" for the nuts of their native lands.

The Navajos of the Southwest

The piñon pine (pinus edulis) is the most important of "nut pines" that grow in this area of the American Southwest. Extremely hardy and drought-resistant, it grows in open stands or scattered groves on the dry foothills.

Piñon nuts are somewhat egg-shaped, less than a half inch long, and, like all pine seeds, are borne under the cone scales. The kernels, rich and distinctively flavored, are encased in thin, brittle shells of a brownish hue. Also called pine nuts and Indian nuts, they have found a ready market in this country for over 40 years.

Most of the commercial crop—about one million pounds annually—is

have also long appreciated the pine nut's food value. Each year, Indian families camp in the desert to harvest them, both for themselves and for the market. The nuts are sold to reservation trading posts, where they are eventually picked up by major processors like WAFCO Distributing Company, Ramies Nut Company and Valley Distributing Company, all of Albuquerque, New Mexico.

Gathering piñon nuts is a popular

autumn sport for others besides the Navajos. Euell Gibbons recalls collecting them as a boy in New Mexico, and in recent years increasing numbers of non-Indian families have been seen gathering piñon nuts for fun and profit in the woodlands of the Southwest.

The piñon pine is a grotesque-looking tree. A veritable mass of deformities, it seldom grows higher than 20 feet, but it can survive conditions that most other trees cannot, including high elevations, periods of drought and temperature extremes. While hardships may stunt its growth and contort its limbs, they don't prevent the piñon from yielding nuts—as many as 30 to a cone and, occasionally, several bushels to a tree.

Since piñon pines are generally short, it is sometimes possible to harvest many nuts from the ground, just by pulling down the branches and twisting off the cones. Occasionally, lucky collectors stumble across squirrel caches containing as much as 15 pounds of piñon nuts. Another technique is to beat trunks and branches with brooms and poles, after first placing blankets under the tree. The result, if the cones are ripe, is a steady hail of nuts. They are then poured into burlap bags. Collectors are paid from 75 cents to $1.25 a pound, depending on market conditions. An advantage of piñon nut collecting, besides the pay, is that so little of the land where the tree grows

is privately-owned—most often, the nuts are yours for the taking.

The pecan, another popular nut, grows wild in the bottomlands of Texas, Oklahoma, Louisiana and other states south of the Ohio River. Texan Alexander Wooldert, a wholesale grocer, is believed to have been the first dealer of wild pecans, at the turn of the century. He also invented the first screw device for cracking the nuts lengthwise, greatly facilitating the marketing of pecans.

The growth of the tourist trade in the South has had much to do with the increased demand for the wild pecan, since much of the crop is sold at roadside stands. Wild pecans are also used in candies and baked goods.

Professional hunters of the wild pecan were paid 25 to 30 cents a pound last year, depending upon "the availability of both the native and hybrid species, which are commercially grown," reports James L. Culpepper of the Louisiana Forestry Commission.

Sassafras Bark

Among edibles with a ready market is sassafras bark, commercially valued since colonial times. It was listed in the "Pharmacopeia Londinensis" of 1618, vying with tobacco as Virginia's chief export. In 1622, the colonists received an order from the Earl of Southhampton for "the sending home of threescore

Sassafras (sassafras albidum) grows in the woodlands and along the roadsides and fence rows from southern New England west to Wisconsin and Iowa, and southward into northern Florida and the Gulf Coast. Often it is not more than a shrub, with honey-yellow flowers blossoming in early spring, and red stalks bearing one-seeded dark-blue fruits in the fall.

thousand weight of sassafras."

So brisk was the trade in sassafras bark in 1625 that one writer of the period complained that London businessmen "bestowe their moneyes . . . upon two commodities onely, tobacco and sassafras—matters of present profitt, but no wayes foundacons of a future state."

According to William Penn, early Pennsylvania settlers put sassafras or pine into their molasses beer. Writer John Josselyn in New England found that boiling root chips in beer made a concoction "excellent to allay the hot range of feavers." American Indians were also convinced of the medicinal properties of sassafras.

When sassafras became an ingredient in popular beverages such as root beer and in proprietary medicines, the demand skyrocketed. As a result, the commercial manufacture of sassafras oil was conducted on a great scale in several eastern states in the late 19th century. In 1883, in Buckingham County, Virginia, 40 distillers were processing 80,000 pounds of sassafras roots each day.

Today, sassafras is still prized for its medicinal properties, particularly by mountain folks of the eastern U.S. who make a spring tonic from it. Others, who place no great store in its contributions to good health, still find that it makes a pleasant and invigorating tea. Sassafras is also of commercial importance as a flavoring and as an aromatic.

Like the piñon pine, the sassafras tree thrives under difficult conditions. It prefers poor soil and can often be found where other trees will not grow—on dry, rocky hillsides and along hard, clay roadside banks. The sassafras tree is usually found where it can get plenty of sunlight—in open areas or at the edges of forests.

Generally considered a weed, the sassafras tree usually achieves only shrub-like proportions, although it occasionally grows to impressive heights. Most stands of sassafras, however, seldom grow large or have trunk diameters exceeding four inches. Two-foot high saplings are plentiful and are harvested by grubbing out the roots with a mattock; a strong, pleasant odor indicates that you have found the right roots. Once taken out of the ground, sassafras roots are scrubbed with a brush and the bark chipped off with a knife. These chips can be stored indefinitely.

Sassafras bark is purchased by the same firms that buy crude drugs (see chapter "Wildcrafting in the Appalachians"). Last year, the F.C. Taylor Fur Company of Louisville, Kentucky, paid $1.40 per pound for the rossed bark of sassafras roots, which can be harvested year-round. Sassafras is unique in this respect, as most wild harvests occur in late summer or fall.

Morel Mushrooms

In northern Michigan, morel mushrooms sprout from the forest floor along with the wild flowers in May. Surprisingly, the collecting of wild morels lures more people into the woods each year than do hunting and fishing, two outdoor sports for which the state is famed.

Hardware stores in towns like Boyne City (the self-proclaimed "Morel Mushroom Capital of the World"), Mesick, Ontonagon, Gaylord, Harrison, Grayling and many others, report a booming business each spring in the sale of every possible type of picking container, including washtubs and garbage pails. In many of these towns, festivals are held to celebrate the morel's appearance.

Many mushroom collectors who descend upon these towns each spring come clear across country to harvest mushrooms, for personal consumption, for the sheer fun of it, or for profit. Buyers at central locations throughout Michigan's upper peninsula purchase bushel after bushel from collectors and ship them to a food cannery in Chicago. Last year, in the Ontonagon area alone "810 bushels of morels were bought from residents . . . and stored in the local freezing plant," according to Mrs. Ingrid Bartelli of the Michigan State University Extension Center.

It seems that the harvesting of wild edibles for market has mushrooming popularity.

The federal and state forestry offices
listed here are good sources of
information for the harvesting of
minor forest products.

REGIONAL OFFICES
OF THE U.S. FOREST SERVICE:

Northern—Federal Building, Missoula, Montana
59801

Southwestern—517 Gold Ave. SW, Albuquerque,
New Mexico 87101

California—630 Sansome St., San Francisco,
California 94111

Rocky Mountain—Federal Center, Building 85,
Denver, Colorado 80225

Intermountain—324 25th St., Ogden, Utah 84401

Pacific Northwest—319 SW Pine St., Portland,
Oregon 97208

Eastern—633 West Wisconsin Ave., Milwaukee,
Wisconsin 53203

Southern—1720 Peachtree Rd NW, Atlanta, Georgia
30309

Alaska—Federal Building, P.O. Box 1628, Juneau,
Alaska 99801

STATE FORESTRY OFFICES:

Alabama—513 Madison Ave., Montgomery,
Alabama 36104

Alaska—232 E. 4th Ave., Anchorage, Alaska 99501

Arizona—402 Office Building E, Phoenix, Arizona
85007

Arkansas—3821 Roosevelt Rd., Little Rock,
Arkansas 72204

California—Resources Building, Sacramento,
California 95814

Colorado—Colorado State University, Fort Collins,
Colorado 80521

Connecticut—165 Capitol Ave., Hartford,
Connecticut 06115

Delaware—E. Tathall Building, Dover, Delaware
19901

Florida—Collins Building, Tallahassee, Florida
32304

Georgia—P.O. Box 819, Macon, Georgia 31202

Hawaii—1179 Punchbowl St., Honolulu, Hawaii
96813

Idaho—State Capitol Building, Boise, Idaho 83707

Illinois—State Office Building, Springfield, Illinois
62706

Indiana—607 State Office Building, Indianapolis,
Indiana 46209

Iowa—300 4th St., Des Moines, Iowa 50319

Kansas—Kansas State University, Manhattan,
Kansas 66506

Kentucky—Capitol Plaza Tower, Frankfort,
Kentucky 40601

Louisiana—P.O. Box 15239, Baton Rouge, Louisiana
70815

Maine—State House, Augusta, Maine 04330

Maryland—Rowe Blvd. and Taylor Ave., Annapolis,
Maryland 21404

Massachusetts—100 Cambridge St., Boston,
Massachusetts 02202

Michigan—Steven T. Mason Building, Lansing,
Michigan 48926

Minnesota—658 Cedar St., St. Paul, Minnesota 55101

Mississippi—1106 Woolfolk Building, Jackson,
Mississippi 39201

Missouri—Box 180, Jefferson City, Missouri 65101

Montana—2705 Spurgin Rd., Missoula, Montana
59801

Nebraska—University of Nebraska, Lincoln,
Nebraska 68503

Nevada—Nye Building, Carson City, Nevada 89701

New Hampshire—State Office Annex, Concord,
New Hampshire 03301

New Jersey—P.O. Box 1888, Trenton, New Jersey
08625

New Mexico—P.O. Box 2167, Santa Fe, New Mexico
87501

New York—50 Wolf Rd., Albany, New York 12201

North Carolina—Administration Building, Raleigh,
North Carolina 27602

North Dakota—State Forestry School, Bottineau,
North Dakota 58318

Ohio—Fountain Square, Columbus, Ohio 43224

Oklahoma—Capitol Building, Oklahoma City,
Oklahoma 73105

Oregon—2600 State St., Salem, Oregon 97310

Pennsylvania—202 Evangelical Press Blvd.,
Harrisburg, Pennsylvania 17120

Rhode Island—83 Park Street, Providence, Rhode
Island 02903

South Carolina—P.O. Box 287, Columbia, South
Carolina 29202

South Dakota—State Office Building, Pierre, South
Dakota 57501

Tennessee—2611 West End Ave., Nashville, Tennessee 37203

Texas—Texas Forest Service, College Station, Texas 77843

Utah—1596 W. North Temple, Salt Lake City, Utah 84116

Vermont—Dept. of Forests and Parks, Montpelier, Vermont 05602

Virginia—P.O. Box 3758, Charlottesville, Virginia 22903

Washington—Public Lands Building, Olympia, Washington 98504

West Virginia—1800 E. Washington St., Charleston, West Virginia 25305

Wisconsin—P.O. Box 450, Madison, Wisconsin 53701

Wyoming—Capitol Building, Cheyenne, Wyoming 82001

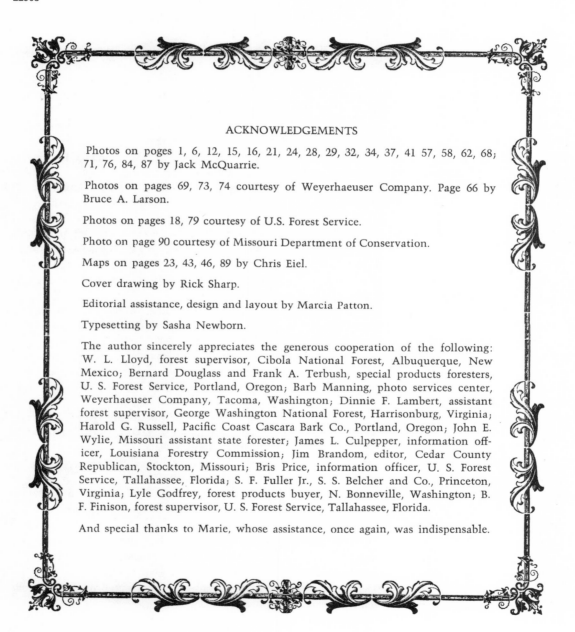

ACKNOWLEDGEMENTS

Photos on pages 1, 6, 12, 15, 16, 21, 24, 28, 29, 32, 34, 37, 41 57, 58, 62, 68; 71, 76, 84, 87 by Jack McQuarrie.

Photos on pages 69, 73, 74 courtesy of Weyerhaeuser Company. Page 66 by Bruce A. Larson.

Photos on pages 18, 79 courtesy of U.S. Forest Service.

Photo on page 90 courtesy of Missouri Department of Conservation.

Maps on pages 23, 43, 46, 89 by Chris Eiel.

Cover drawing by Rick Sharp.

Editorial assistance, design and layout by Marcia Patton.

Typesetting by Sasha Newborn.

The author sincerely appreciates the generous cooperation of the following: W. L. Lloyd, forest supervisor, Cibola National Forest, Albuquerque, New Mexico; Bernard Douglass and Frank A. Terbush, special products foresters, U. S. Forest Service, Portland, Oregon; Barb Manning, photo services center, Weyerhaeuser Company, Tacoma, Washington; Dinnie F. Lambert, assistant forest supervisor, George Washington National Forest, Harrisonburg, Virginia; Harold G. Russell, Pacific Coast Cascara Bark Co., Portland, Oregon; John E. Wylie, Missouri assistant state forester; James L. Culpepper, information officer, Louisiana Forestry Commission; Jim Brandom, editor, Cedar County Republican, Stockton, Missouri; Bris Price, information officer, U. S. Forest Service, Tallahassee, Florida; S. F. Fuller Jr., S. S. Belcher and Co., Princeton, Virginia; Lyle Godfrey, forest products buyer, N. Bonneville, Washington; B. F. Finison, forest supervisor, U. S. Forest Service, Tallahassee, Florida.

And special thanks to Marie, whose assistance, once again, was indispensable.